Excelsior

The Racing Years

Paul Ingham

Published in 2011 by Ilkley Racing Books
3 Mendip House Gardens Curly Hill Ilkley LS29 ODD

Excelsior: The Racing Years ISBN 978-0-9524802-8-0

Printed by The Amadeus Press, Cleckheaton, West Yorkshire

Editor: Raymond Ainscoe

Front cover: Norman Webb at Muckamore corner, in the 1950 Ulster Grand Prix.
(Courtesy of News Letter Sport)

Rear cover: Svend Sorensen's Swedish Grand Prix winning 1934 Excelsior Mechanical Marvel which was subsequently raced by Ivan Wickstead at Brooklands.

About the author:
Paul Ingham has been a vintage motorcycle enthusiast all his life, racing a 250 cc Excelsior Manxman in the vintage class during the late '70s and restoring and collecting old motorcycles ever since then.

This book is number 427 of a limited edition of 500

ACKNOWLEDGEMENTS

This book has been some years in the gestation and I would like to thank the people who have helped with support and information, as follows:

Dave Hiron, whose uncle Tom Wildman was the racing workshop foreman at Excelsior, giving Dave a lifelong interest in the marque. Dave has been a most helpful source of enthusiasm and information in the book's preparation.

Allan Sorensen, whose father is a major feature in this book. Allan has kindly allowed me to use photographs from the family albums and has relayed the stories told to him by his father.

Raymond Ainscoe for kick-starting me into writing the book after years of talking about it and for helping with its preparation.

The editor of "Classic Racer" magazine, Malcolm Wheeler, from Mortons Media Group Limited, who is an enthusiast of anything built for racing, and who has allowed me to use scans of various photographs and articles in the Mortons archive.

My wife Sylvia who has put up with motorcycles ever since we married and who has always been supportive of my hobby gone mad.

Tracey, my daughter, who has been working the computer, moving photos etc., and generally stopping me wiping everything off with one stroke of the wrong key.

Bill Shaw, my old friend from Knuzden in Lancashire, who started me off with Excelsior Manxman motorcycles.

Justin Broughton of ABACUS Communications who has helped with all the technical work.

A special word for Jackie McCredie. Jackie was for many years the oldest surviving TT competitor and, during the course of the book's preparation, in 2009 he kindly wrote the Foreword. He passed away on 25 May 2010 at the grand age of 102. My only regret regarding this book is that Jackie did not survive to see it published.

There are many others who have contributed information and photographs and I thank them all. In the event that a photo has not been appropriately credited, the copyright holder is invited to contact the publisher.

This book is just a taster; if it is successful, a full history of the marque is proposed. If you have information or photos which you would like to be considered for use in such a publication, please contact me at excelsior-manxman.co.uk or via the publisher.

Paul Ingham
Cumbria,
April 2011

FOREWORD

I am delighted to provide a few words about Excelsior motorcycles, as the highlights of my racing career were associated with the Manxman. I was fortunate enough to own two Manxman racers, which I rode in eight Lightweight TT races, from 1939 to 1953. And, in 1952, my Manxman carried me to my best international result: third in the 250 cc class of the North West 200, behind the legendary Arthur Wheeler on his ex-works Moto Guzzi.

I am very pleased that, nearly 80 years old, both my Manxman racers survive intact, together with the four bronze replicas which they and I won at the TT.

Like the TT, I have passed the 100 mark, but I well remember the great stars of the 1930s, particularly my friend and fellow Scot, the legendary Jimmie Guthrie. And I still remember the apprehension of heading down Bray Hill for the first time on my Excelsior. All the experienced mountain circuit riders were assuring me that they took it flat out but I did not dare. It was only after some laps that I realised that they were having me on. Only a handful of top riders, like Stanley Woods, did that in my day.

On my 100th birthday, a cherished present was a photo of me riding my Manxman through Parliament Square, Ramsey; it brought back many happy memories. I hope that you find this book and its photos convey the atmosphere of Excelsior's important part in the story of those far-off racing days.

Jackie McCredie
Edinburgh 2009

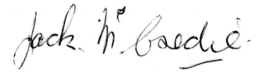

Jackie at one of his local meetings in Scotland

T F Sinclair entered the 1923 Lightweight TT on this super Excelsior fitted with a Blackburne engine.
Unfortunately he retired in the race.

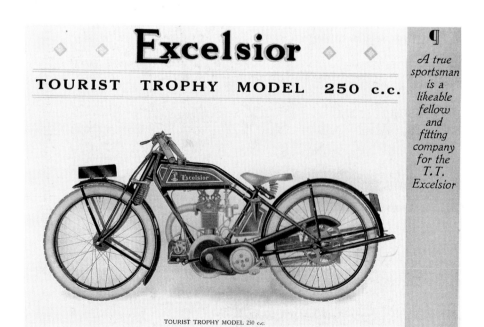

¶ A true sportsman is a likeable fellow and fitting company for the T.T. Excelsior

For £62 the 250 cc Tourist Trophy Model could be yours in 1925.

THE J.A.P. ENGINED RACERS

C.S. Staniland raced this potent 350 cc Excelsior Brooklands special in 1927. (*Courtesy of Richard Jones; source unknown*)

1929 was to be the year of the marque's first TT win. Syd Crabtree astride the winning 250 cc Excelsior JAP with the managing director of the Excelsior Motor Company holding his hat. *(Mortons Media Group Archive)*

Factory photo of the TT bike for 1929; special features include the four speed hand change Burman gearbox operated by two levers and Webb 8" racing hubs. Four bikes were entered in the 1929 Lightweight TT, ridden by S.A.Crabtree, L.C. Crabtree, J.H.Blackburn and L. Higson. Syd Crabtree won with an average speed of 63.87 mph; J.H. Blackburn came twelfth; the other two factory entries retired. *(Norman Webb collection)*

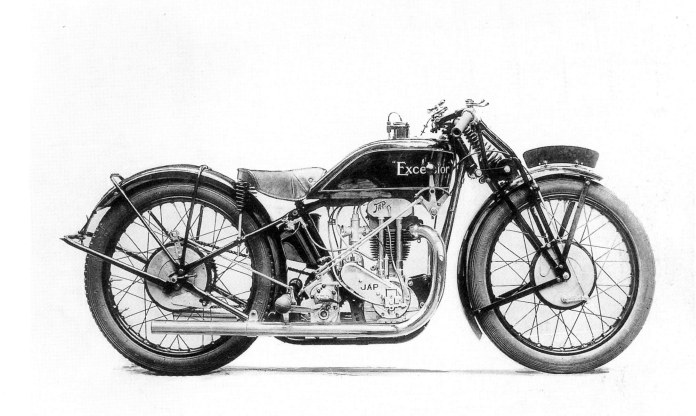

This photo shows one of the surviving 1929 TT bikes. The gearbox was modified to a Norton dolls head type and various other alterations were made to keep the bike competitive. The metal on the petrol tank is wafer thin to save weight.

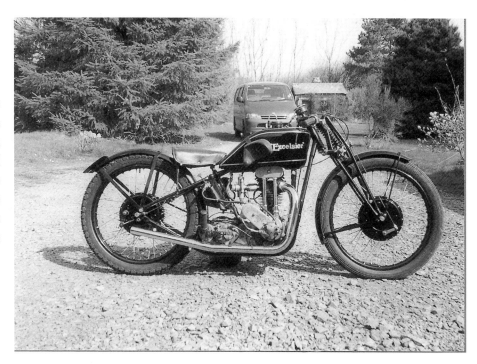

This is a factory shot of the works 1930 250 cc TT Excelsior JAP racer.
(Norman Webb collection)

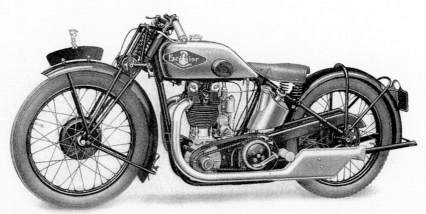

THE 1929 T.T. WINNER

Excelsior

Famous since 1874

250 c.c. ISLE-OF-MAN Special

TOURIST TROPHY
MODEL No. 13

The actual machine which won the Lightweight 1929 T.T. (the fastest ever run) at Record Speed.

WINNER OF
1928
Dutch T.T., German, French, Belgian, European and Brooklands Grand Prix.
1929
Dutch T.T., French and Brooklands Grand Prix and LIGHTWEIGHT T.T. at Record Speed and 41 FIRSTS and WORLD'S RECORDS at Brooklands.

£78 : 0 : 0   250 c.c. ISLE-OF-MAN SPECIAL TOURIST TROPHY MODEL No. 13

22

From the Excelsior brochure for 1930: the TT Model No 13 was offered for sportsmen.

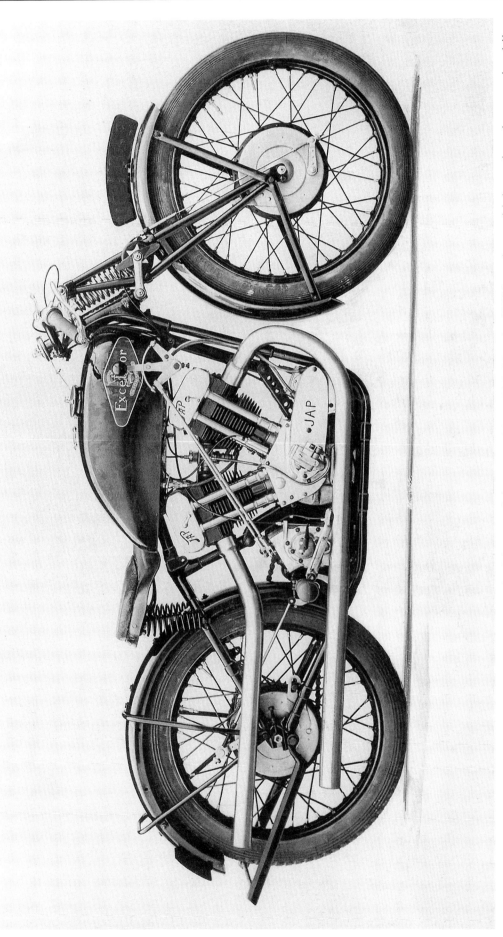

For the 1930 TT Excelsior went for something special with one of the new 500 cc JAP V twin OHV engines which produced a stunning bike. Syd Crabtree retired from the Senior race when in 12th place at the end of lap 5. Cotton and OK Supreme also had JAP V twin entries but they too retired. *(Norman Webb collection)*

Two 500 c.c. T.T. engines—a single and a twin—undergoing comparative tests on Heenan and Froude brakes.

Photo of the V twin on engine brake at JAP prior to the TT.

A feature in the press prior to the TT, describing the motor.
(*Mortons Media Group Archive*)

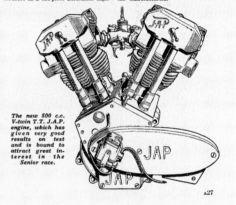

J.A.P. ENGINES FOR THE T.T.

IT is a long time since there was a V-twin in the T.T., but J. A. Prestwich and Co., Ltd., have produced an engine of this type of 500 c.c., which has shown up very favourably on the test bench, and which it is confidently hoped will do well in the Senior next month. Although it is, of course, a new departure, and is therefore bound to be regarded as something of an experiment, there is every reason to expect it to put up a good performance, and it is certain to arouse enormous interest.

The engine consists, with very few modifications, of two 250 c.c. single-port racing cylinders, set at 50 degrees on a special crankcase, which follows closely the design of the larger twins. In appearance it is an extremely good-looking engine, and in capabilities we are told that at a speed of something over 6,000 r.p.m. it develops considerably more than 30 b.h.p.

The dimensions are 62½ mm. bore and 80 mm. stroke, the timing gear is of the four-cam type and is practically a smaller edition of the 8-55 h.p. engine. A double Best and Lloyd oil pump, used in conjunction with the well-known J.A.P. system, in which a rotary release valve is employed, delivers lubricant to the main bearings, the front cylinder and the rocker gear, while an independent supply feeds the valve guides.

The connecting rod and big-end assembly is a very pretty piece of work; of the forked type, the connecting rods are made of deeply grooved girder-section steel, machined and polished all over. In the forked end is a fixed steel sleeve, upon which the single-ended rod is free to rotate on a bronze bush of large diameter. As the relative motion here is only a rocking motion, this is entirely adequate. The sleeve itself, which carries, of course, both rods, rotates about the crank pin on a four-row roller bearing, the full length of the pin, the rollers being mounted in a one-piece duralumin cage.

There are—up to date—20 J.A.P. engines entered in the Lightweight, eight in the Junior and eight in the Senior races. The makes using the 500 c.c. twin are Excelsior, Cotton and O.K. Supreme. Although there is still a month to go before the races, 30 T.T. engines have already been dispatched to the manufacturers.

The new 500 c.c. V-twin T.T. J.A.P. engine, which has given very good results on test and is bound to attract great interest in the Senior race.

A27

A surviving PTOR 500 cc racing JAP engine; this one was supplied to Chris Tattersall of Blackpool, who built it into a chassis and raced it a couple of times. He wanted JAP to fit twin port heads back and front to use at Brooklands, and they refused, so he removed the engine and used it as a doorstop! On his death the engine was sold to another gentleman in Blackpool who also used it as a doorstop. It is now used to hold a radiator up!!

Syd Crabtree on a 1931 works bike. The only major race I have found him winning that year was the Dieppe International held on 27th July, so perhaps the photo is at Dieppe. His brother L.C. Crabtree is standing behind him. (*Source unknown*)

JOE WRIGHT   20-11-1931   SILVER COMET

J.S Wright, the Brooklands rider, with his V twin Excelsior JAP "Silver Comet" which he hopes will take him to a new world record. *(Source unknown)*

548　　　THE MOTOR CYCLE　　　*APRIL 28th, 1932.*

A Supercharged Single

How a Powerplus Blower has been Arranged to Supercharge a 500 c.c. J.A.P Engine

FOR some months past the J.A.P. concern has been experimenting with the problem of supercharging a single—a type which does not lend itself kindly to such experiments; they appear, however, to have been extremely successful. A 498 c.c. Excelsior-J.A.P. has been fitted with a standard vane-type Powerplus blower, fitted between carburetter and engine, and tests have been made at Brooklands. M. V. McCudden was to have ridden the machine at the April 16th meeting, but the event has been twice postponed owing to the weather and, since no all-out tests have been made at the time of writing, the full capabilities of the machine are an unknown quantity; bench-tests, however, have shown a b.h.p. figure of 50 at 6,000 r.p.m. The compression ratio of the engine (unsupercharged) is 8 to 1.

McCudden, who is to ride it, with the complete Excelsior-J.A.P.

The accompanying drawing clearly shows how the blower has been mounted in extensions of the front engine plates. The mounting is an eccentric one to provide for adjustment of the chain.

The Drive

This chain is of the same dimensions as the primary-drive chain, and transmits power from a seventeen-tooth sprocket on the end of the crankshaft to a twenty-four-tooth one on the blower; this gives a ratio of roughly 1.4 to 1. A sturdy cam-type shock-absorber takes the drive from the blower sprocket to the shaft.

Undoubtedly the most interesting feature of the design is the fact that two carburetters are used. One, the main instrument, is a standard T.T. Amal, mounted low down in front of the crank case and feeding mixture to the blower. The other is a " baby " Amal feeding into the induction pipe near the port, and is employed only for starting purposes. The control of the two instruments is independent, by a single lever in each case.

The engine is started up on the small carburetter, and, when it has warmed up, the throttle of the small carburetter is shut and the larger instrument brought into use. The throttle slide of the " baby " carburetter has to be a very close fit, since it must resist the considerable pressure in the induction pipe at high speeds.

Once on the main carburetter, the engine can be opened up. A by-pass valve in the induction pipe allows a certain amount of the gas to escape into the open air at low speeds. This valve is interconnected with the throttle, and is shut off when a speed of about 70 m.p.h. is reached.

The whole layout is neat, and the only pipe, apart from the induction and fuel pipes, is the lead to the blower oil pump, mounted on the off side of the casing. Since the engine is set well back in the frame the weight of the blower, it is stated, makes no noticeable difference to the handling.

BROOKLANDS SWAMPED AGAIN

Third Time Lucky?

BROOKLANDS has been unlucky with the weather again. The April 16th meeting had to be postponed until Wednesday of last week, but the elements merely repeated their performance of the previous Saturday; they did relent sufficiently to let the track dry, but not until it was too late to run the meeting. So another postponement has been made—until May 7th (2.30 p.m.). Will it be a case of third time lucky?

A 18

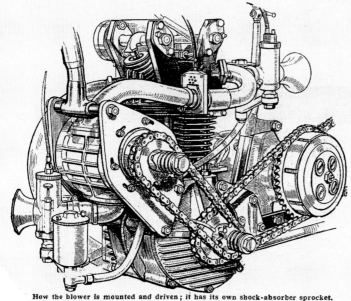

How the blower is mounted and driven; it has its own shock-absorber sprocket.

"Power Plus Blower has been arranged to Supercharge" a 500 cc Excelsior JAP. Mr McCudden was hoping to ride the machine at Brooklands. *(Mortons Media Group Archive)*

The photos show TT4, a works 500 cc Excelsior from late 1931. This was welded under the seat tube rather than bolted up. I bought this bike about 20 years ago with the intention of restoring it but never got around to it. The bike was worn out and had been ridden in to the ground. A later Burman box from the late '30s had been fitted at some stage and the rear end turned into swinging arm. This bike had a very large pistol grip type tank similar to the New Imperial works job but larger and mounted differently.

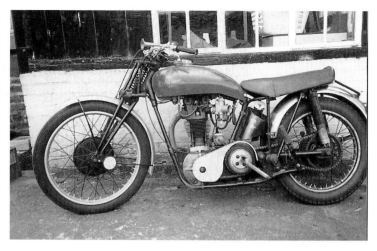

The only time I have seen photos of an Excelsior with a tank like this is in the book "A Clubman at Brooklands" by A.C. Perryman on page 33, featuring D.J. Pirie in the Brooklands Senior Grand Prix, 23 July 1932, on his 498 cc Excelsior JAP. He was also entered the same year in the Manx Grand Prix in the September; unfortunately he retired after completing two laps, with water in the magneto.

The log book was not issued until 1941. The registration number JPH 963 was issued in Surrey between September 1940 and April 1942. This would suggest that the bike was used unregistered for racing up until the War and put on the road later. I did a deal with Brian Angliss who at the time ran Autokraft at Brooklands. Brian had the rear end put back to rigid but, before he finished the bike, Autokraft went into receivership. The bike then appeared in the Autokraft receiver's sale at auction. It was a pity that I had no money on that day as the bike brought £2,700 less than I originally paid for it.

(Photos from the Paul Ingham archive)

Eric Fernihough was doing well at Brooklands and other races with Excelsior motorcycles
fitted with JAP engines. (*Mortons Media Group Archive*)

Eric Fernihough's two JAP 175 cc engines on the
shelf in Norman Webb's bedroom.
(*Norman Webb collection*)

A JAP test sheet for a 350 cc IOR racing engine of the period.

ENGINE **JAP** DETAILS

TYPE **350 cc. O.H.V. Racing**   SYMBOL **"IOR"**

BORE M/M **70** STROKE M/M **90** "A.C.U." RATING H.P. **3·45**

OVERALL DIMENSIONS ..... HEIGHT INS. **20½** DEPTH INS. **9⅝** BREADTH **9¾** OPEN **13¾** FRONT. **13¾** REAR. **12⅜**
   " M/M **520** " M/M **244** " M/M **247** **349** **313**

WEIGHT .... NET LBS. **68** COMPLETE WITH MAGNETO, CARB., ETC. **75 APPROX.**

TIMING COVER & DRIVE... OPEN **YES** FRONT **YES** REAR **YES (LOW & HIGH)**

BEVEL **X** SPECIAL

BEARINGS .... **¼" x ¼"** BIG END **ROLLER** **¼" x 5/16"** DRIVING SIDE **ROLLER** **¼" x ¼"** TIMING SIDE **ROLLER**

PISTON .... MATERIAL **ALUM^N MC·1** TYPE **DOME TOP** RINGS **·3 x 1/16" WIDE**

INLET PIPE .... OUTSIDE DIA. FLANGE CARBURETTER **"AMAL" 45·A · "BINKS" 45·B**

   CARBURETTER

EXHAUST ~~PIPE~~ PORTS ..... OUTSIDE DIA. **2"** TYPE **PLAIN** VALVE No. **X**

DRIVING SPINDLE .... MAX. DIA. TAPER **·747** TAPER 1 IN 8 x **11/16"** SCREWED 26 WHIT. X **9/16"**

CHAINLINE .... ENGINE C.L. TO MAX. DIA. OF TAPER **2⅞"** GEAR BOX **3" (76 M/M)**

~~CHAIN~~ GEARBOX: **"BURMAN"** **3·SPEED "T" 3 PLATE** **4·SPEED "C" 3 PLATE**

SPARKING PLUG ... RACING **TOURING** **A-C 5·4 G·1** **"LODGE" H·45 BR·29** **"KLG" 246 348**

MAGNETO (ANTICLOCK.) **"M-L" CMA· "BTH" M·1· "LUCAS" MA·1 · "BOSCH" FF1·A**

FUEL .... **"ROAD" 25% TO 50% PETROL/BENZOL · TRACK · DISCOL RD·1· OR PMS·2·**

LUBRICATION ·............... **CASTROL "R" DIRECT FEED TO BIG-END.** **ROTARY VALVE**

REVS. P.M. & AVERAGE B.H.P. **2800/** **3200/** **3600/** **4000/** **4500/** **6200/ 22**

TOP GEAR RATIO NORMAL... SOLO **5·25 TO 1** SIDECAR **6·5 TO 1** ENGINE SPROCKET **TEETH ¼" OR 5/16" WIDE** **SOLO SIDECAR**

ESTIMATED ROAD SPEED... **DEPENDS ENTIRELY ON CONDITIONS** SOLO M.P.H. SIDECAR M.P.H. ENGINE SPROCKET **PITCH. ½" ROLLER. ·335**

TIMING .... INLET VALVE **B/TDC OPENS 3/16" OR 24°** CLOSES **A/BDC 39/64" OR 55°**

WORK TO DEGREES
FOR PREFERENCE

EXHAUST VALVE **B/BDC OPENS ¾" OR 62°** CLOSES **A/TDC 13/64" OR 25°**

CRANKCASE RELEASE... OPENS **B/BDC 65°** CLOSES **A/BDC 25°**

MAGNETO **B/TDC ADVANCE 15/32 TO 5/8"** CENTRES **35 M/M**

COMPRESSION .... VOLUME **57-58 cc** RATIO **7·3 TO 1 · 7 TO 1 WITH 1/16" PLATE** **" " 1/32" "** **7·7 TO 1 " NO "**

DRAWING No. **1222.**   J. A. PRESTWICH & Co. LTD.,
    TOTTENHAM, LONDON. N.17.

Fernihough, July 1934, at the Brooklands circuit. *(Mortons Media Group Archive)*

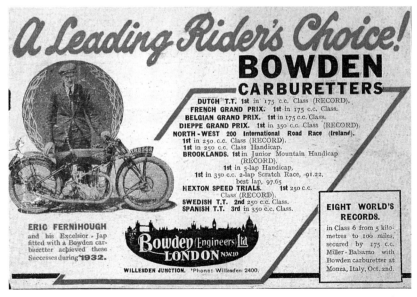

Bowden was promoting its products with Fernihough using their carburetters.

Harold Warburton, garage proprietor from Blackpool, who was an Excelsior factory rider in both the JAP and Manxman eras

C.D. Reich at the start of the 1934 Senior Manx GP, 498 cc Excelsior. Unfortunately the bike packed up on the second lap of the Mountain. *(Courtesy of Keig Photography, Isle of Man)*

A shot of Tom Wildman on the left. He must not have been working quickly enough as the hammer is being offered as an alternative.

For the 1932 season the racing 500 cc Excelsior B14 was introduced. Having seen one of these bikes race, it is clear that the engine has considerable power and the bolt up frame has a hard time keeping everything in line.

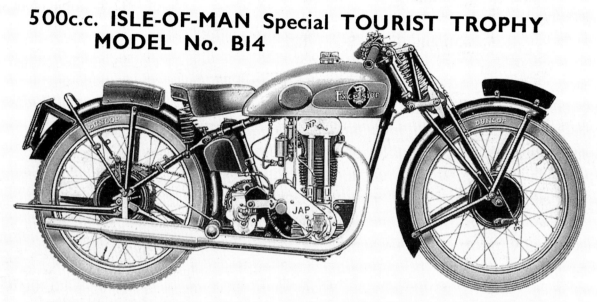

500c.c. ISLE-OF-MAN Special TOURIST TROPHY MODEL No. B14

This Model is outstanding in Performance having a maximum speed in the region of 100 m.p.h.

SPECIFICATION

ENGINE.—Jap 80 × 99 single port **SPECIAL** Racing Engine. Roller bearing big end, roller bearing pulley side, special aluminium piston, return springs to rocker gear, roller bearing rockers. All rockers and push-rods enclosed. Mechanical lubrication incorporating sight feed. Oil pump driven off engine. The big end in this engine has two rows of rollers in phosphor bronze cage, and is identical to the engine which has put up such phenomenal speeds in English and Continental road races this season (497 c.c.).

FRAME.—New design frame of exceptional strength, giving great stability and low riding position, as used with great success in the T.T. and Continental Grand Prix races.

FORKS.—Special racing model forks, incorporating hand controlled shock absorbers, forged steel links, and taper tubes, etc.

GEAR.—Burman three-speed close ratio racing gearbox, with hand controlled clutch and footchange.

TANKS.—Latest design extra strong all steel saddle tank, petrol capacity 3 galls. Separate oil tank, oil capacity 4 pints. Chain lubrication incorporated in the separate oil tank. Chromium plated finish, quick release filler cap exactly as used in T.T.

CARBURETTER.—Large racing Amal carburetter is fitted as standard. With twist grip controls.

WHEELS.—Racing, built up with 10-gauge spokes. and fitted with Dunlop 27 × 3 ribbed front and 27 × 3 studded rear.

SADDLE.—Best quality supple top racing type.

BRAKES.—Extra large 7″ internal expanding front and rear. Forged steel drums, with wide shoes, giving enormous braking effect.

TRANSMISSION.—By heavy Coventry chains, $\frac{1}{2}″ × \frac{5}{16}″$ and $\frac{5}{8}″ × \frac{1}{4}″$.

MUDGUARDS.—"D"shapeguards,of ample strength and width. With flat steel stays.

HANDLEBARS.—These are fitted by a special clip to the steering head, are adjustable and fitted with racing twist grips and outside levers.

STEERING DAMPER.—This is of approved design, and easily adjustable.

KNEE GRIPS.—These are permanently fitted as standard, and are adjustable to suit riders' convenience.

SILENCER.—Chromium plated straight-through exhaust pipe, with detachable round sports type silencer of large dimensions, which can be readily dismantled for cleaning.

EQUIPMENT.—Kit of tools, inflator, chain punch, and Tecalemit grease gun.

WEIGHT.—278 lbs. (approx.).

Price No. B14 - - - - - £69 : 0 : 0

Model No. B14, 500 c.c.—*Code Word:* "Racpor."
"Racporlite" with lighting set.
EXTRAS'—See special column.

HIRE PURCHASE TERMS :
Initial Payment £18 0 0
12 Monthly Instalments of 5 3 6
Insurance included in H.P. amounts.

This B14 has matching engine and frame numbers. By the latter end of 1932 the Albion four speed box was offered as an alternative to the standard three speed Burman box. This bike is fitted with one of the Albion gearboxes.

(*Paul Ingham archive*)

The Excelsior JAP racers were coming towards the end of their production but, if you look in the periodicals of the time, Excelsiors with JAP engines were still entered at all the big events taking records and providing privateers with a competitive bike for years to come. Some bikes were still racing in the '80s.

GRAHAM W. WALKER, G. H. TYRELL - SMITH, G E. NOTT and W. L. HANDLEY wore the "Litesome" Body Belt in scoring their amazing run of 1930 successes.

Photos by permission of "The Motor Cycle."

Even the factory riders needed some support!
(*Mortons Media Group Archive*)

C.J.P. Dodson in the 1932 500 cc TT being chased down by Nott on a Rudge who passed him for 4th place. Dodson finished 5th   *(Mortons Media Group Archive)*

This 500 cc B14 was bought new by R. Stobart in Cumbria and entered for the 1932 Manx Grand Prix. Unfortunately he retired with a puncture at the end of lap one. One interesting feature was the fact that the engine was one of the few made with return sump, which it still retains.

I saw it many times trying to tie its self in knots going up Barbon Hill Climb. It was still owned by a member of the Stobart family until 2010. The top end had been altered to the late speedway type, but the original "dog ear" head is with the bike (shown below). The bike is now with only its second owner, other than the Stobart family.

Postcard of Cyril May on an Excelsior B14 with return sump engine. The postcard says "West Wilts Motor Cycle Club". This bike has had its wheels modified from standard.

A. Macintosh on a C14 in 1936 with a full return oil system. He was better known as H.A.R. Earle and he was the winner of the Motor Cycle Trophy for the best performance by a clubman at Brooklands. This bike still exists.

(*Mortons Media Group Archive*)

THE MARVEL

Eric Walker, the managing director, decided that Excelsior should have its own racing engines so he commissioned Burnley and Blackburne to design something special. Ike Hatch came up with what is now known as the 250 cc Mechanical Marvel. This was an OHV radial four valve head with a central spark plug, two splayed downdraft inlet ports and twin exhausts. The camshafts were located high up at the front and rear of the crankcase, and the barrel was sunk deep inside the crankcase and the magneto was operated via a skew gear and had vernier adjustment. The head and barrel were held down by four bolts straight through from the crankcase. TT Amal carburetters (sic) were fitted.

Four bikes were entered for the 1933 Lightweight TT to be ridden by Cecil Barrow, Sid Gleave, Wal Handley and Syd Crabtree. The race unfolded as follows:

Lap 1: Handley was in the lead, Gleave and Duncan (Cotton) were tying for second, Crabtree was lying fifth and Barrow had dropped out with engine trouble.

Lap 2: Gleave had taken the lead, Handley was second and Crabtree fifth.

Lap 3: Handley had dropped to third.

Lap 4: Crabtree was down to sixth.

Lap 5: Gleave still led and Handley was up to second and Crabtree fifth.

The final lap: Handley's engine put him out at Sulby and Gleave came over the line the winner with an average speed of 71.59 mph and the fastest lap of the race, being his third at 31mins 11 secs. Crabtree came home in fifth.

Walter Handley racing the Marvel in the 1933 TT.
(Mortons Media Group Archive)

S. GLEAVE. EXCELSIOR 1st 1933 Lwt TT. 71.59 m.p.h.

The engine came straight out of the box and won the TT with Syd Gleave aboard. Second place went to Charlie Dodson (New Imperial, No 8).(*Mortons Media Group Archive*)

Walter Handley giving it some hammer at Ramsey hairpin trying to catch Syd Gleave.
(Mortons Media Group Archive)

Advertisement for winning the TT

What happened to the 1933 TT winning bike?

For sure, this bike was broken up. At the end of the 1933 season the Marvel chassis was re-designed with a new welded up frame, new style petrol and oil tanks, different hubs etc.. The only remaining original parts were the engine, gearboxes and forks that were assembled into the new chassis.

Alan Bruce stated in a letter to Norman Webb that he was given one of the old 1933 chassis into which he fitted a JAP engine for Horton to use in the 1934 Senior TT. It is also known from Alan Bruce's letter that the TT winning engine was one of the two that went over to the Swedish GP in 1934.

It is my own opinion that the other three 1933 chassis would have been re-enamelled and sold off with JAP racing engines fitted. Parts have surfaced from time to time. For instance, Norman Webb found some Marvel cycle parts and built up an engine from spares, to create a Marvel which is now on display in the National Motorcycle Museum. And in the last twelve months an original Marvel 1933 tank has been discovered in Gloucester.

A nice period shot of two 1933 Marvels – Syd Gleave on the left and Leo Davenport on the right.
(Norman Webb collection)

The re-designed Marvel for the 1934 season in its silver and red livery. (*Norman Webb collection*)

(Norman Webb collection)

On joining Excelsior, Alan Bruce brought with him a special twin magneto 500 cc racing JAP engine built especially for Excelsior. This was to be the factory's final tilt at the 500 class using a proprietary engine. The 1934 TT was to be the showcase for this bike. Unfortunately the worst happened when Syd Crabtree, entered on the 250 cc Marvel, was killed in the Lightweight TT. Ted Mellors had taken the 500 out for a couple of laps in practice earlier in the week so he was allowed to take it over for the Senior but he retired after two laps.

There was a second 500 factory entry using a JAP engine ridden by K.N. Horton, who crashed on the first lap at the 33rd milestone breaking his ankle. *(Courtesy of Keig Photography, Isle of Man)*

THE SENIOR T.T. EXCELSIOR
Featuring Twin Mags. and a New Carburetter

June 13th 1934

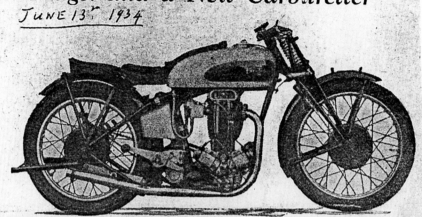

EXCELSIORS are racing a machine in the "Senior" fitted with their own engine, which has many original features. Alan Bruce, the Australian, who has many clever designs to his credit and is still the holder of the world's sidecar speed record, has been responsible for this and it reflects considerable credit upon him.

The bore and stroke are 80 mm. and 99 mm., giving 498 c.c. The compression ratio is approximately 7.4 to 1, the cylinder head is aluminium-bronze, while the barrel is cast iron to which alloy fins are shrunk.

Bowden

Prayer-book float chambers, one of which is here shown partly cut away, are a feature of the novel carburetter fitted to the big Ex. It is adjustable to any induction slant.

Six holding-down studs are employed. The overhead valves are push-rod operated, the rods being enclosed in tubular cases. The popular down-draught induction system is utilized and the single exhaust pipe is attached to the cylinder by a finned ring.

Two Sparks.

The most unusual feature is that two magnetos are used. Identical B.T.H. magnetos are synchronized and driven by bevel gears from the camshaft.

The 14 mm. Lodge plugs are located one between the push rods and the other exactly opposite it on the near side. This dual ignition arrangement has been found to have a number of practical advantages.

Dry-sump lubrication is provided, and the triple Pilgrim-type pump has one lead direct to the big-end, another to the timing gear, main bearings and

Mechanically, the Senior Excelsior to be ridden by Syd. Crabtree is one of the most interesting jobs in the Island. Largely "fathered" by Alan Bruce, it has an exceptionally thorough lubrication system and twin magnetos and sparking plugs.

cylinder wall, while an auxiliary feed is taken to the rockers and valve guides; all operate under pressure.

A rev. counter, also driven from the

A rev. counter dial is sunk into the Excelsior tank top, and the Sorbo-rubber pad is securely fixed in position.

camshaft, is sunk flush with the 4½-gallon fuel tank, and this will be retained for the race. Incidentally, it is of interest to note that the maximum useful revs. are in the region of 5,500.

The driving side of the main bearing consists of four rows of caged rollers, both the timing side and the big-end having two rows of rollers, also caged. The crankcase is heavily finned and the flywheels are steel stampings—excep-

tionally light ones for a road racing 500 c.c. job.

The frame is an enlarged edition of that used on the 250 c.c. machine, the "Mechanical Marvel," which won the Lightweight race last year with Syd. Gleave riding.

The Albion four-speed gearbox is, of course, foot operated, and the top gear will be in the region of 4.4 to 1.

Harwill 8-in. brakes are employed and the front and rear tyre sizes are 26 ins. by 3.00 ins. and 27 ins. by 3.25 ins. respectively.

There is a one-gallon oil tank on saddle tube from which run exceptionally large bore pipes; a Dunlop saddle with a Sorbo top, high tensile steel rims, light steel mudguards, and Webb racing forks. The latter are half an inch longer than usual in order to provide greater ground clearance.

This new Excelsior looks a very workmanlike job and should give an excellent account of itself in the race.

No Irish End-to-end.

The Ulster Centre of the Motor Cycle Union of Ireland has decided not to run the Irish End-to-end Reliability Trial. It had been arranged to revive the event in July, provided 30 entries were received. The number has fallen far short of the figure fixed, so the event is therefore off for another year.

Write up of the one-off 500 cc TT bike. *(Mortons Media Group Archive)*

Drive side of the works 500 1934 bike that Crabtree was to ride in the 1934 Senior TT, that was subsequently taken out by Mellors. I love this shot with the gentleman holding up the sheet whilst having a cigarette

Ted Mellors on the factory 500 after taking over the Senior TT ride that Syd Crabtree was to have ridden.

The twin magneto 500 Excelsior. Later in its life the engine was acquired by Norman Webb. I bought the engine off Norman and eventually it went to Brian Angliss at Autokraft where it was fitted into an appropriate chassis. It is now on display at the National Motorcycle Museum.

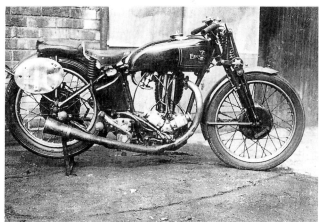

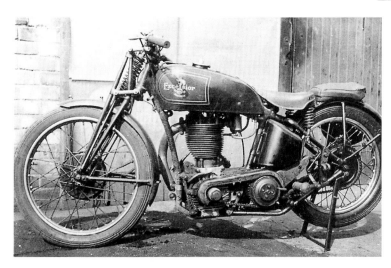

(Norman Webb collection)

Alan Bruce joined the Excelsior company just after Easter 1934 and was given the title of Team Manager for the TT and the forthcoming Continental Circus season. On arrival four bikes were being built for the forthcoming TT, and a fifth bike was supplied to, and entered in the race by, the dealer Cecil Barrow.

According to a letter from Alan Bruce to Norman Webb written in 1980, the engines had been looked over by Eric Fernihough and, while Eric was in hospital, his apprentice Francis Beart had drilled through the masked plug holes to allow the plug to show through on all four engines. The original heads took bottom seating plugs and you put a washer in first for the plug to sit on, and a small hole broke through the chamber to allow the spark to do its work.

It seems the first time anybody knew about Beart's work was when Mellors, having been issued some bottom seating plugs by Eric Walker whilst testing a bike at Donington, changed plugs because of a misfire and eventually it packed up.   Apparently Eric Walker was present when the head was removed and it was discovered that the valve was slightly bent and the plug was sticking through the head. Eric was furious as, whatever the rights or wrongs, he had not given his permission for Beart's revision.

The masked head was designed for a purpose and, with the hole drilled out, although the engine may have performed well flat out on the Brooklands mile, it did not accelerate well and oiled plugs at the TT.

Before this episode Fernihough had enjoyed a free run at the factory but, after a meeting with Eric Walker, Fernihough was never seen at the factory again according to Alan Bruce. The Marvel engines were expensive and Excelsior had paid for the development as well as the engines themselves.

At the TT Syd Gleave had trouble with plugs oiling after the run down Bray Hill as he rolled back the throttle to avoid over revving. Next day Alan Bruce was present in the pits; when Gleave pulled in they checked the long reach plug and found that it was oily. A short plug was fitted and Syd reported the engine was stutter free for the rest of the practice laps.

Alan Bruce recalls in his letter that he and Tom Wildman worked all through the night finishing off the spare bronze head to be fitted to Syd Crabtree's TT bike as he was Eric Walker's principal rider. But the TT was a disaster for the team; Crabtree was killed, Gleave finished sixth and the others retired.

The centre of the cylinder head – you can see that the plug hole is not drilled all the way through. The shot of the spark plug shows the little washer that sits between the head and the spark plug.

Excelsior's race shop in the Isle of Man, 1934. In the background, left to right: Horton, Tom Wildman, Alan Bruce bending on the second machine. In the foreground, two unknown mechanics, a fitter from the brake lining company and Syd Gleave. *(Mortons Media Group Archive)*

Svend Aage Sorensen

Svend Sorensen was born in 1903 in Taarnby, Denmark, and lived there until he died in 1980. He was a major feature of the Excelsior racing scene.

This photograph shows some of the prizes he won.

His father had a cycle shop and then moved to new premises in Copenhagen, two streets from where Svend opened his own shop in 1936.

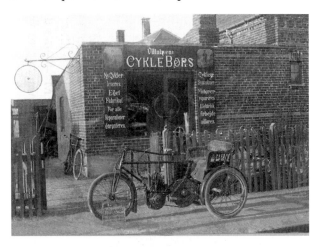

(Courtesy of the Sorensen family)

Sorensen was entered in the 1934 Swedish Grand prix at Saxtorp on a Mechanical Marvel. Alan Bruce wrote that an engine was assembled from all the best parts of the TT engines and built into a chassis, The only other alteration was the colour change from Marvel silver with red panel to black with red panel; whether this was done out of respect for Syd Crabtree or if they were thinking ahead for the proposed Manxman that Alan Bruce was developing we will never know. Eric Walker handed Svend an iron engine to be used for practice to save the bronze motor for the race. How can you not smile having been given one of these to use?
(*Courtesy of the Sorensen family*)

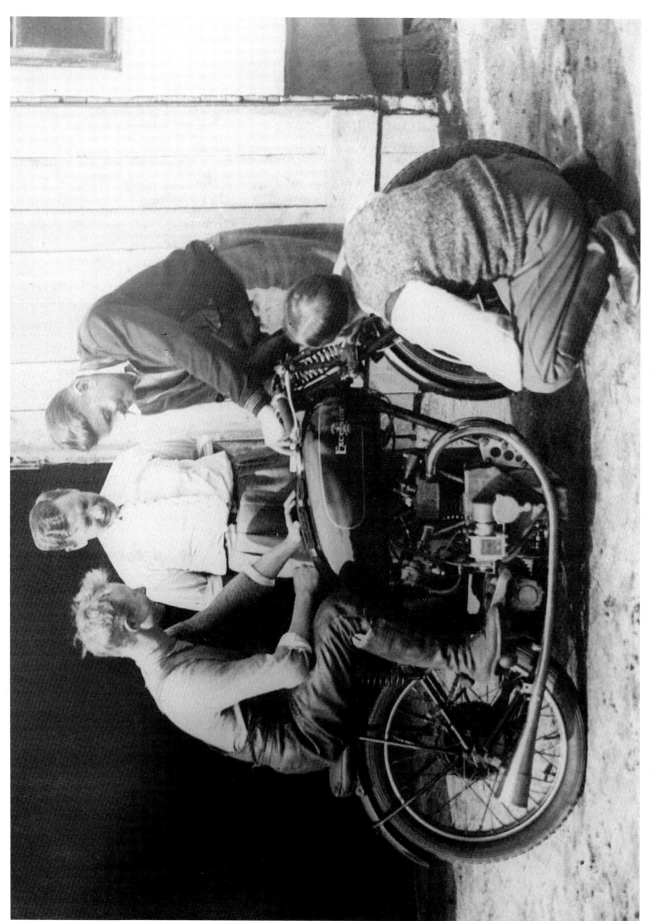

Sorensen sat on the bike and Alan Bruce gives some advice. *(Courtesy of the Sorensen family)*

Svend Sorensen flat out
with the Marvel

The three winners at
Saxthorp, left to right:
Mellors – Junior;
Sorensen –
Lightweight;
Sunnqvist – Senior.

The trophy for winning the 1934 250 cc Swedish GP is still with
Svend's son Allan who was named after Alan Bruce.

Seen at Brooklands, looking grave but confident: Ted Mellors, and the Mechanical Marvel Excelsior he will ride in the Lightweight T.T.

(*Mortons Media Group Archive*)

Mellors in action at Ramsey Hairpin in the 1934 TT.

For the rest of 1934 the Marvel squad took in the Continental Circus with results as follows: in the Dutch, Mellors was fourth and Davenport fifth; in the Swiss G P Mellors was second but Gleave and Charlie Manders both retired. Mellors was again runner –up in the Belgian GP with Leo Davenport a retirement. The Dieppe GP saw a win for Mellors and another a retirement for Davenport. There were victories for Mellors and Fernihough in the Leinster 200 and the Brooklands Clubman Race respectively.

In 1935 the Marvels started getting into private hands as Excelsior concentrated on the Manxman racer. Dennis Parkinson ended up with a Marvel and had a second at Donington and retired in the Manx. R.J. Edwards entered the 1936 Manx on a Marvel but retired on lap one. (He also had a few rides on a CTS.)

The Sorensen Marvel came back from winning the Swedish GP and passed into Ivan Wickstead's hands. With Winslow as the tuner in the backroom Wickstead raced it throughout the 1935 season. (Winslow's journal is a fascinating insight and record of the Marvels, but it will be saved for a more in depth book.) Wickstead won at Brooklands.

BELOW: After winning his first race, Ivan Wicksteed poses astride the 250 c.c. Excelsior which carried him to several victories at Brooklands in 1935. The machine was known as the Mechanical Marvel.

(Mortons Media Group Archive)

The bike then passed on to W. Whipps who rode the bike at Brands Hatch but Whipps reported to Norman Webb that the bike was not at ease over what was essentially a dirt track. The bike was overhauled by Excelsior in either 1937 or 1938 and entered in the 1939 Manx which was cancelled. Whipps emigrated to Canada and left the bike with a friend who it was sold for him after the war.

A Marvel racing at Brooklands in April 1937 with Francis Beart at the controls. *(Mortons Media Group Archive)*

Marvel Memorabilia

Cigarette card of Mellors featured in the Kings of Speed series by W.A. & A.C. Churchman

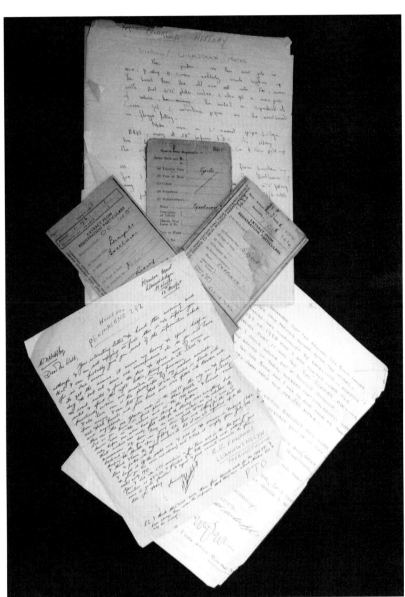

Photo of original Marvel log books, also letters from former Marvel riders Edwards and Whipps and the Winslow/Wickstead racing notebook.

Norman Webb bought out what was left of the Excelsior race shop; they still had a new set of machined crankcases in 1955. These, Norman told me, are what he used on the built up 1933 bike.

Norman Webb with one of his Marvels in the garden.

The fire at the National

The lucky thing was that most of the Excelsior racing bikes were in the foyer and saved from the fire. One Marvel was in the racing hall and ended up burnt. I was asked to restore the bike as I am an Excelsior fan and had bought all Norman Webb's racing spares.

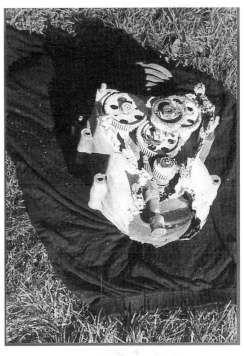

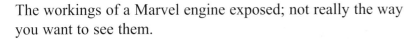

The workings of a Marvel engine exposed; not really the way you want to see them.

I had the bike restored within the 12 month period that Roy Richards asked for; there were tears in his eyes on delivery. The bike can be viewed in the National.

Ronnie Mead, the well known road racer, worked for Bill Webster from Crewe. Websters were Excelsior agents and also had a large stock of pre-war Manxman parts. Ronnie decided to run a Mechanical Marvel in the 1947 TT but his bike had blown up in the Leinster 200. It was reported in the press that Ronnie had to work 18 hours a day for 12 weeks to get the bike ready for the TT. Telescopic forks were fitted and the rigid back end was converted to swinging arm. A Grand Prix New Imperial rear wheel was fitted.

Ronnie's luck was against him with the little bike as, in the paddock, an ambulance backed into the bike, also fracturing Mead's toe, so that he was unable to compete.

At the time of writing the engine is being refurbished to running order. The bike will be seen at events on the Continent and will soon be on display at the Hockenheim museum.

This engine is currently being prepared by Gernot Schuh of www.vintage-motoren.at in readiness for the bike's first demonstration outing on the track for perhaps 60 years.

Norman Webb restored three of the Marvels and was most of the way on with the 1933 type bike before he became ill. I am not sure but I think this restored Marvel in the photo must have been displayed on the 1958 Excelsior Earls Court stand as a letter from Eric Walker in 1960 refers to him returning Norman's photo taken two years earlier.

Norman pointing out something to the two Walker brothers and Sorensen third from the left
(*Norman Webb collection*)

THE MANXMAN

After the 1934 TT according to Alan Bruce's letter to Norman Webb, Eric Walker offered him the position of Technical Manager which was to cover design and development. He was set up in a secret office and nobody other than the company directors and secretary were to know what he was up to.

Bruce was of course busy drawing up the new frame for the new racer, the Manxman. Again Burnley and Blackburne were to supply the engines. Excelsior paid for the patterns and design. The Manxman was to replace the Marvel which was regarded as overly complicated to be sold to the public.

Alan Bruce's job was to come up with the chassis. The first one was visually like the 1934 Marvel but with a cradle for the engine to sit into; obviously the dimensions were altered and on the road bikes the rear frame under the seat was bolted up. The factory racing Manxman kept the welded frame under the seat. This became a standard feature on the production racers later.

Norman Webb, who knew Sorensen, said that Sven liked the bolted up frame so, even though he was an unofficial works rider, he did use the bolted up frame as well as the welded type.

Alan Bruce was given authority to choose one rider to race an experimental machine in 1935. He selected Charlie Manders who won the 250 class in the North West 200 and finished sixth in the Lightweight TT. For 1936 Tyrell Smith and Ginger Wood were to join the team.

R.M. Board using one of the old 1935 works bikes in the 1936 Manx Grand Prix. He completed only two laps. *(Courtesy of Keig Photography, Isle of Man)*

One of the factory Marvels at rest

A nice shot to show "out with the old and in with the new". Saxthorp 1935: Sorensen number 78 is now mounted on the new Manxman with the old Marvel on the same grid.

This is one of my favorite shots - Charlie Manders on the left with a full 1935 works welded frame Manxman and Sorensen no 78 on a works bolted frame bike. Special features on the engines are the elektron cases and a strengthening web on the crankcase front; this did not go in production for the public until 1938 on the BRBR Series. Not a bad old New Imperial in the background. (*Courtesy of the Sorensen family*)

Nice group of riders at Saxtorp in 1935; from the left: Sorensen, Stanley Woods, Manders, Aage Wagner, Alan Bruce in the back and Tyrell Smith.

The start of the 1935 Saxtorp Grand Prix

These photos were forwarded from Australia and many thanks. This is the Charlie Manders bike that finished sixth in the TT in 1935. Bill Spence bought this bike at the 1939 TT along with the Excelsior syndicate 500 bike. Both were taken to Perth and then mothballed during the war. Both were raced, and won, at the Victory TT in Western Australia in 1946.

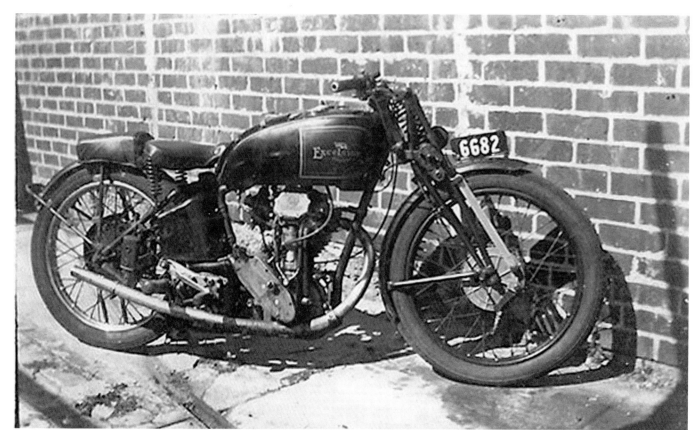

Sorensen opened his own motorcycle shop in 1936 as shown in the above 1938 photograph, and of course became an Excelsior agent.

Headed envelope as Excelsior agents

Always happy to entertain!

How to get there and what to do when you are not watching the racing!

Jackie McCredie

Jackie McCredie's first Excelsior was a BRAR model on which he first ventured to the Isle of Man, finishing thirteenth in the 1939 Lightweight TT, despite an excursion along the tarmac. His second Excelsior, a late works plunger model, is shown in the photo. This bike started life as a factory rigid entry for F.S. Cadman in the TT and Ulster GP of 1938, registering a retirement and a fourth place respectively. For some reason the bike was produced in the old Marvel silver and red colours. The bike then went to Thompson of Greenock, whose brother Alan won the Scottish 250 speed Championship in 1939 and 1947.

Charlie Brett then acquired the machine and it went back to the factory to have one of the two spare sets of works rear springing rear ends fitted. Jackie McCredie bought the bike from Charlie Brett, changed its colour scheme and used it to finish fourth in the North West 200 and thirteenth in the TT of 1949. In 1952 he came third in the NW 200, nineteenth in the TT and tenth in the Ulster.

The bike later won the Southern 100 and then ended up with Dick Isles at Whittaker Motors at Blackpool. The bike still exists in a private collection, very much as it was when Jackie raced it.

McCredie's ex-works 1938 plunger BRBR Manxman. (*Dick Isles collection*)

A pre-War shot of Jackie McCredie, no 73, on his early rigid BRAR Manxman, taken from the inside of Clady Corner at the Ulster, chasing no16, one of the works Excelsior semi-unit bikes.

(Courtesy of News Letter Sport)

Jackie McCredie at Quarter Bridge on his ex-works plunger Manxman in the 1952 Lightweight TT.

This nice shot taken on the outside of Clady corner at the Ulster showing McCredie's no12 ex-works Manxman leading no 27, an REG motorcycle blowing a bit of smoke out. (*Courtesy of News Letter Sport*)

ALL COMMUNICATIONS TO BE ADDRESSED TO THE COMPANY AND NOT TO INDIVIDUALS

The
**EXCELSIOR MOTOR
COMPANY LIMITED**
(Prop. of BAYLISS THOMAS & CO. Est.1874)
**KINGS RD., TYSELEY,
BIRMINGHAM, 11.**
SERVICE DEPT.: REDFERN ROAD

DIRECTORS:
R. ERIC WALKER, M.B.E., M.I.B.E.
REGINALD WALKER   (MANAGING)
GEOFFREY E. WALKER, M.I.B.E.
D. A. WALKER
TELEPHONE NUMBERS:
ACOcks GREEN 1677-8-9
TELEGRAMS:
"MONARCH" HAYMILLS

CONTRACTORS TO ALL GOVERNMENT DEPARTMENTS

YOUR REF   OUR REF

REW/JB

6th Sept. 1948.

Mr. J.McCredie,
11 Wilfred Terrace,
Edinburgh 8.

Dear Sir,

     We have pleasure in enclosing herewith our cheque for
£22. 7. 0. in respect of your racing successes, made up as follows :-

T.T.	Renold & Coventry Chain Co.	£5. 0. 0.
	Dunlop Rubber Co.Ltd.	£7. 7. 0.

Grand Prix d'Europe
     Renold & Coventry Chain Co.   £10. 0. 0.

     Please accept our combined congratulations and best wishes
for the future.

     Yours faithfully,

     pp. EXCELSIOR MOTOR CO. LTD.

     Managing Director.

Letter from Eric Walker concerning McCredie's bonuses for 1948. Interestingly Jackie had totted up on the bottom left everything for the year and it comes to £160-17 shillings - not bad when the average weekly wage was £3-18s (£3.90 today)!

Sorensen's 350 cc bike had now appeared on the scene.

Sorensen and his friend Agner Hansen.

Sorensen congratulated by Lassen Landorph after his win in a Nordic championship race at the Amager trotting track in 1934.

By 1938 a very special bike came available for Sorensen to use at selected meetings. The factory had come up with the semi-unit spring rear end bikes for the factory team; it also produced one pre-unit rigid bike. The semi-unit bikes were going to be sold to the public in 1939 and even were shown in the 1939 catalogue but Eric Walker put a stop to this when he realised that the factory was to be put on war production. The bike for Sorensen had all the special features of the springer such as ribbed hubs, Girling cable brakes, new shape petrol tank, lighter forks, different wheelbase, oil tank mounted forward of the seat tube to aid oil cooling; the list of special features just goes on and on…...

Sorensen with the new bike

Sorensen behind no 85, wondering if he should be lending the factory bike
to Villy Jorgensen

Villy wondering how much this will cost if I crash it!

I just had to put this shot in; I love the pit
attendant's hat.

Stanley Woods and Sorensen at Assen with the new bike.

Assen - Sorensen looks just about all in

RACING SPECIFICATION:

BOTH MODELS can be supplied in Racing trim at £10–0–0 extra, including the following racing specification :—

Aluminium **bronze** head with polished ports.
Special **racing** valves and springs.
Special racing cams and high compression racing piston.
B.T.H. or LUCAS racing magneto. No lighting set.
Special **racing** carburetter.
Close ratio four-speed gear.
Gears and Shafts of K.E. steel.
No kickstarter.
DUNLOP **racing** saddle with **sponge rubber** pad on top of tank.

T.T. mudguards with rear guard pad, **racing** position footrests, and brake pedal.
T.T. type chromium plated **steel chain guard**, with lubrication to front chain by **adjustable drip feed.**
7" T.T. Brakes, with **special alloy shoes.**
27"×2.75" Ribbed or Studded DUNLOP **racing** front tyre, and 26"×3.00" **racing** DUNLOP Studded rear tyre—both with **security bolts** and **well fillers.**

NOTE.—ALL "**MANXMAN**" MODELS are delivered suitable for running on 50/50 Petrol-Benzol fuel.
A **rev. counter** graduated to 8,000 and with **built-in drive** to engine positively lubricated can be supplied for flush fitment in top of tank at an extra charge of **63/-**. (Sixty three shillings).

Back at the Excelsior factory the Manxman racers were getting under way. This ultra-rare pre-production supplementary brochure is in the making, with some of the specifications pencilled in. Note the vertical shaft top and bottom bevel housings are not what were used on the bikes and are changed in the production sales catalogue. None of the catalogues can be relied on for exact specifications.

Alan Bruce meanwhile was getting to grips with the 1936 works racing bikes; they now had a re-designed 4 valve o.h.c assembly. There was in fact a little brass tab on the head showing the Rudge four valve patent.

This shot shows Tyrell Smith after finishing in second place in the 1936 TT on one of the new racers with an average speed of 72.51mph. Alan Bruce far left *(Courtesy of Keig Photography, Isle of Man)*

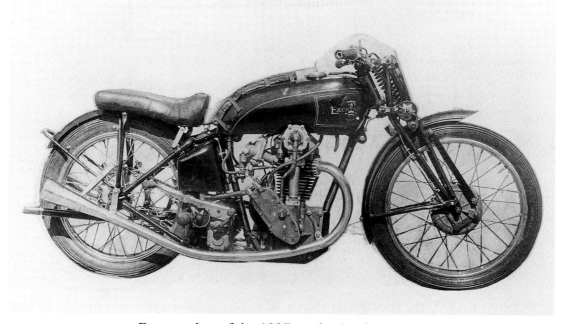

Factory shot of the 1937 works 4 valve racer.

Drive side of the 1937 works 4 valver.

Tyrell Smith flat out, the timing side shown (*Courtesy of Keig Photography, Isle of Man*)

Tyrell Smith on the 4 valver in the 1937 TT, chasing Tenni. (*Mortons Media Group Archive*)

1937 was set to be another great TT. Tyrell Smith set off at a great speed and on the last lap was 5 seconds behind Tenni on the Guzzi. Unfortunately the con-rod let go at the Creg. Ginger Wood was 3 min 12 seconds behind at the start of the last lap; he put in a superb lap to end up in second place just 37 seconds behind Tenni. This photo shows Alan Bruce, the team manager, shaking Ginger's hand and Tom Wildman, the race shop foreman, at the back behind Bruce. (*Mortons Media Group Archive*).

20-4-1938.
GINGER WOOD NO 23
250 4 VALVE MANXMAN.

Ginger Wood, no 23, at the start of the Donington April 1938 meeting, on a works 4 valve Excelsior. Ginger ended up second to Maurice Cann on a Guzzi. Also in the race you may spot L.J. Archer (New Imperial), J.J. Booker (Royal Enfield), D Parkinson (Excelsior), Ron Harris (New Imperial), R Pike (Rudge) and other famous names.

DUNLOP
Jubilee International
Motor Cycle Races
Donington Park
AUG 27th 1938

SOUVENIR · PROGRAMME · SIXPENCE

Donington programme from later in the 1938 season.

The "over the counter" bikes were doing very well all over Europe and at home and Alan Bruce in one of his letters to Norman Webb said that "It was not realised that in 1937/8 Excelsior built as many racers as Norton".

This is a nice period shot of BRAR 110, originally bought by R.S.Simpson via Kings. Frame number MRG215 indicates that it was built in the second half of the series, as it has the large seat with the upright seat fixings rather than the single saddle fitted to the earlier bikes. This was later owned by Freddie Hawken and went back to the factory to have rear plungers fitted. Sparrow became the next owner and the bike went on to Norman Webb. At some period a later series BRBR engine, no 121, was fitted and the records show that this was built from bits by Tyrell Smith in 1947. The bike can be viewed in the National Motorcycle Museum.

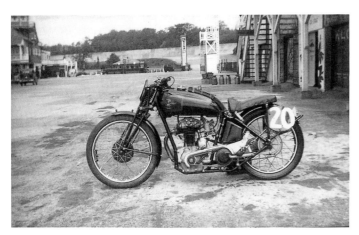 

These are photos of a late racer being delivered new at Brooklands, before and after race tuning

Alan Bruce, back at the factory, was building the bikes for the 1938 race season. By reason of financial constraints the 1937 engines were stripped down to get the elektron crankcases. He had designed a plunger rear suspension, and the new gearbox was now bolted direct to the back of the crankcase. He also tried a swinging arm system but decided that, as the semi-unit engine and the special cradles to house them were well advanced, it would require a complete engine/frame re-design to get the geometry correct for the swinging arm version, so this project was shelved. These plunger bikes were in the 1939 catalogue and we know that Brassington ordered one for the Manx and was not very happy when only a rigid turned up in the Isle of Man.

Nine sets of plungers were ordered: three for the works 250 bikes, three for the 350 bikes, one for the 500 and the two spare sets were sold and fitted to the Brett and Hawken bikes in 1947. Two one-off bikes were also made, a semi-unit rigid and the pre-unit rigid.

Ginger Wood on the works pre-unit bike for 1938, later given to Sorensen.

Charlie Manders on the short 1938 semi-unit rigid bike. (*Courtesy of Keig Photography, Isle of Man*)

The team was entered in the 1938 Lightweight TT and won the Manufactures Team Prize. Ginger Wood was second; Tyrell Smith came in third and Manders fifth. The Club team award also went to the three works Excelsior riders for the Dublin and District M.C.C.. Maurice Cann who was fourth, on a private Excelsior, took the Newcomer's Award.

Excelsior had eight finishers in the race and three retirements which was not bad, considering a lot of the bikes were home-prepared.

Photo of the team that won the Prize: left to right, Tyrell Smith, Charlie Manders and Ginger Wood. Behind them with the flat caps are Tom Wildman wearing his official arm band on the right and Alan Bruce on the left.

TT programme for 1938 and the team medal.

Lo Simons of the Netherlands was one of the top riders on the Continent and always had something special and a works engine. Shown below at Assen in 1947 where the 250 cc and 350 cc classes were run together, Lo finished fifth.

(Courtesy of Mr van Brecht)

(Courtesy of Motor Rijwiel)

Jaap Zwaal was second in the Dutch Championship 350 class
in 1938.
Photo kindly provided by his son. (*Source unknown*)

Dennis Parkinson

As can be seen in the previous pages, the privateers with racing Excelsiors were featuring in all the big events.

W.H.Parkinson was a motorcycle dealer in Wakefield who held the Excelsior agency.
For 1936 his son Dennis had one of the latest works type frames with a BRAR engine fitted. He went out and won the Manx Grand Prix. For the next year he was lent a factory prepared engine, BRBR100, for use in the Manx. This engine was fitted with hairpin head and valve springs, as was the development engine BRA100S.

Both these engines were taken to the TT in 1937 as works practice motors and in fact Sorensen started the Lightweight race with engine no BRBR100 but he retired. The engine was next used by Manders in the Dublin100 race but he too retired. The engine was rebuilt and tested time and again and then lent to Dennis Parkinson as a works engine for the Manx. This was strictly against the Manx regulations but these things happen.

(Just a note as something to watch for when buying a race engine: BRBR100, a development engine, and BRBR101/S, the 1938 show bike, were the start of the late number series. But, at the time, the newly designed crankcases were not finished and it is not until BRBR102 that we start with high lug position crankcase that people expect with the bronze hairpin head motors. A quick look distinguishing feature is that the front engine plate is flat on top "frame to case" whilst, on the later modified engines, the top of the engine plate has to slope upwards towards the barrel. Information from Tom Wildman's factory notebooks)

Again for 1938, after his 1937 Manx win, Parkinson was given something special as was Jack Worswick. Both had thinly disguised works semi-unit bikes.

In Roland Pike's book he mentions that "The hot Excelsiors in the 1938 Manx were the ones that were ridden by Worswick and Parkinson who, all the riders knew, were factory supported." In the end they were three mph faster per lap than the next man and four mph faster than the next Excelsior.

Parkinson, 1937 Manx Grand Prix winner
(Courtesy of Keig Photography, Isle of Man)

Parkinson on the 1938 bike
(Courtesy of Keig Photography, Isle of Man)

J. A. Worswick in the top shot came fifth in the Manx Grand Prix on the rigid bike in 1937. For 1938, below, he had a semi-unit works bike, the same as Parkinson, and came home to second place. Worswick was tipped to win the 1939 Manx but the war broke out and he became a pilot flying Lancaster bombers; he completed 35 missions and on the 36th mission, on 12 June 1942, he was shot down and lost his life. He was awarded the DFC posthumously. *(Courtesy of Keig Photography, Isle of Man)*

Excelsior never did run a works team again after 1938.

In April 1939 the Ministry of Supply inspectors arrived at Tyseley to give instructions regarding re-tooling as Excelsior was to be engaged in defence production. Almost overnight the racing programme was cancelled and Alan Bruce and Tyrell Smith were virtually out of work.

They concocted a plan; Eric Walker agreed to sell them the late works bikes and what spares they needed for them to run in the TT; they also had free use of the race shop and test bed. The tanks were all black to distinguish them as the "syndicate".

The "syndicate" bikes outside the Coventry workshop; left to right:
No 44 the Manders 250;
No 12 the Manders 350;
No14 the Tyrell Smith 500;
No 30 the Tyrell Smith 350;
No7 the Tyrell Smith 250;
No 10 at the end of the row, the Sorensen 250; and in the middle without a number the Sorensen 350.

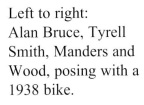

Left to right:
Alan Bruce, Tyrell Smith, Manders and Wood, posing with a 1938 bike.

The 1939 TT:

The Senior
The new 500 pre-unit bike was entered. The bike did not have the pace and Tyrell Smith was only ever as high as eleventh before he retired on the sixth lap.

The Junior
Manders retired on the first lap with gear trouble at Bray. On the second lap Sorensen was touched at the bottom of Bray Hill by H.B.Waddington and brought off. Tyrell Smith, after coming off in Ramsey Square on the first lap, re-started but managed only thirteenth place.

The Lightweight
This was a better race for the syndicate; unfortunately Sorensen retired at the end of lap one still suffering the effects of the fall in the Junior. Tyrell Smith managed third, the first British bike home after the Benelli of Mellors and the DKW of Kluge. Manders came home in sixth place

Excelsior advertising their places

The Tyrell Smith 500 that was taken over to Australia
(Courtesy of Keig Photography, Isle of Man)

This shot shows Sorensen at the start of the 1939 Lightweight TT. You can see the leathers are scuffed on his shoulder and backside where he bounced on the road in the earlier Junior race.

Comparison of works racers

The years 1938/9 were the pinnacle of development for racing motorcycles before the War put a stop to such things. The photo overleaf shows the semi-unit works bike that was raced by the factory in the 1938 TT then lent to Worswick for the Manx and again run in the 1939 TT by the syndicate. The second bike is the works 250 cc Benelli. The engine is the 1938 unit fitted into the 1939 supercharged chassis but other than slight timing cover changes was the same as the bike ridden to victory by Mellors in the 1939 TT. This bike itself did compete in the 1938 and 1939 TT. These two bikes were at loggerheads and contenders at many events; how do they compare?

Manxman

Elektron cases, cam box timing covers and oil pump, alloy head and barrel. Short movement plunger suspension. Semi-unit engine with elektron four speed gearbox, racing special Webb girder forks, cable operated Girling brake in Harwell special ribbed hubs, steel tanks and one piece seat Amal carburetter.

The Benelli

All alloy engine fitted with outside flywheel semi-unit with a bolt up alloy gearbox, girder forks, swinging arm suspension working inside plunger boxes, damped externally by finger controlled dampers, alloy tanks 7" brakes with alloy hubs finned for cooling with a wide brake contact area and, for long distance races, an external oil cooler was fitted. Benelli's own make carburetter 38mm.

The Riders

Benelli - Mellors was the No 1 works rider and had previously raced Marvels for Excelsior. Dickwell, whose bike is shown in the photo, was, like Sorensen, a favoured works rider.

Excelsior - 1938 Ginger Wood, Manders and Tyrell Smith. In 1939, Tyrell, Manders and Sorensen. Tyrell Smith was Excelsior's No 1 rider but Ginger Wood had equal ability, with Manders and Sorensen not far behind.

In the 1939 TT, Tyrell came third behind Mellors on his Benelli and a second place DKW.
When the bikes were weighed in after the race, the DKW was the heaviest at 316 lbs, then the Benelli at 291 lbs and Tyrell Smith's Excelsior at 283 lbs.

The Excelsior company built the works racers to win but Eric Walker was a businessman and the road bikes looked like what was racing so this perhaps constrained the development programme somewhat. We know that by 1938 he had withdrawn development funding with an eye to the looming war.

From the left; McCredie's two bronze replicas, Syd Gleave's TT wining trophy, Ginger Wood's second place silver replica for the 1938 Lightweight, then Norman Webb's two bronze replicas. In the centre are the 1938 team medals.

Showing the art work used throughout the 1930s by Excelsior

Experimental and works parts

Experimental engine built by Alan Bruce but never put into production

Last type of factory racing alloy head and barrel. Note the rear drain on the head which went directly to the sump. Other interesting features are Lucas magneto with elektron body and experimental Amal flat slide carburetter.

Some interesting parts used in the works engines

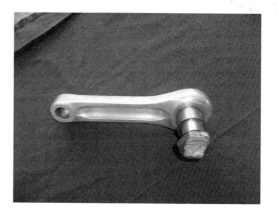

- Vertical shaft and bevels with the roller bearings built in, fully adjustable top bevel housing to save shimming.
- Plain bearing big end running directly on the conrod
- Elektron components to save weight.
- The special piston waisted underneath the crown.

After the War

Once the War was over there was no more works racing department so the factory bikes passed into private hands. Tom Wildman carried on helping the racing men and appeared at the race meetings as the face of Excelsior until the factory finished servicing the racing bikes. When Norman Webb finally bought out the contents of the race shop and the experimental parts, he had already become a major collector as well as a racer.

Dave Hiron's uncle Tom Wildman played a major part at Excelsior. Dave still has his uncle's photos and paperwork which have provided a valuable insight so I have added a few shots of Tom who seems to have been a modest sort, keeping himself in the background.

A postcard from Ben Drinkwater to Tom thanking him for help. Uncle Tom in the background as usual, right hand side.

Alan Bruce left, Tom centre and Ginger Wood holding the bike.

Tom right at the back outside the team hotel in Douglas in the late 1940s or early 1950s.

Two shots after the war with Tom Wildman in the race shop helping the lads. We think this is Freddie Hawken with him but are not sure. It is certainly the Hawken bike that they are working on, with the plunger rear end. There are an ex-factory unit plunger on a bench, an AJS 7R and one old works rigid Excelsior in the shot.

(Dave Hiron archive)

Tom Wildman (far left), Norman Webb (with his leg in plaster after a horrendous spill) and Svend Sorensen.

Sorensen entertaining the crowd at the TT.

Sorensen's son Allan called this car "the Smuggler". It seems Sorensen drove from Denmark with the Norton on the back and the lightweight Manxman inside with the wheels tied anywhere they would fit. England still had rationing and full salami and dried sausage were hidden inside the tyres of the spare motorcycle wheels to give to Tom Wildman when he stayed with him and friends.

Norman Webb

My old friend Norman Webb was an avid collector of racing motorcycles, and when I first got to know him he must have owned 50 to 60 genuine racing motorcycles, many of them works models. He was racing these bikes after the War when there were no new racers available and, especially in the 250 cc class, the old factory bikes were still reasonably competitive.

By the mid to late '50s he had bought out all that was in the Excelsior race shop and was in the enviable position of knowing where most of the proper, now obsolete, works racers were languishing. For the following 20 years or so he set out with a passion to collect as many as he could.

I heard a story of him camping outside someone's house for three days persuading them to sell an Excelsior and I can well believe this tale, as a visit to Norman's house was very enjoyable but took a minimum of six hours.

Norman was also friendly with one of the Benelli brothers. He had a passion for this marque and was offered a factory one-off ride, and at one time owned four genuine works double overhead camshaft Benelli racers. He related that he went to the factory in Pesaro and was given, free, all he could fit into his van!

If it were not for Norman and the other collectors of the time, most of the pre-war works bikes and their history would have been lost. Most of the display of Excelsior racers at the National Motorcycle Museum in Birmingham at one time formed part of Norman's collection.

The shots on the following page are of Norman in his racing days on the Manxman racer showing parts of the Isle of Man TT course and the Ulster.

Norman arriving for the 1949 Lightweight TT with one of the old factory semi-unit plunger 250 cc bikes.

Norman at Ballaugh Bridge in the 1949 TT.

1949 TT and Norman is just ahead of R Edwards on a CTS.

Norman, no 97, in the 1950 TT leading a pack down Bray Hill.

1951 TT: Norman, no 18, chasing down Sparrow on the ex-Freddie Hawken plunger Manxman. *(Mortons Media Group Archive)*

Practice in the 1951 TT: Reg Armstrong, AJS 7R, and Norman. *(Mortons Media Group Archive)*

Norman motoring through
Quarry Bends in the 1950 TT

Norman at the Ulster in 1950, number 101, just up the inside of a Grand Prix New Imperial.
(Courtesy of News Letter Sport)

Modernising the machine

As time passed, riders tried to keep their pre-War bikes updated, fitting swinging arms, telescopic forks etc. Sorensen was no exception and fitted a Norton featherbed chassis with a Manxman engine for a competitive 250.

He was rather worried what Norton would say about the conversion as he had recently been presented with a medal by the factory inscribed "To an old and tried friend" but there was no ill-feeling.

These two shots show a late series BRAR 250 cc Manxman. This engine was dyno tested 30/7/1937 and the bike is one of only three that have come to light so far with matching engine and frame numbers.

The bike went to Czechoslovakia and at some stage has been updated with a plunger conversion that is of an unknown make. The rest of the bike is exceptionally original, even down to the strengthening straps on the oil tank and under the mudguards.

It is thought that this bike was the inspiration for Jaroslav Walter, later of CZ fame, who produced his own engines and then bikes.

This bike is on display in the Hockenheim museum.

This Excelsior engine, owned by Norman Webb, had been fitted into a Garden Gate chassis and, with a KTT Velocette tank atop, it was used in the 1951 Lightweight TT.

Photo outside Norman's garage with the white sheet behind.
(*Mortons Media Group Archive*)

BRBR103. This matching engine and frame bike had a rear end conversion fitted to keep up with the times. This bike still exists and the current owner has put it back to rigid.

TT legend Bill Smith on the Earles alloy framed Manxman special ridden in various events
by J. Sparrow

The 1938 Show Bike.

In April 2009 Bonhams announced their April auction and there were three or four lots of Excelsior bikes/parts. On first inspection Lot 368 seemed to be a bit of a mess but, on closer viewing, Dave Hiron and I found some fascinating features. There was an original test sheet signed by Alan Bruce and Ginger Wood, headed "Show finish", and the engine and frame numbers matched. The racing gearbox end cover was in another lot with the proper number matching the test sheet. All the Excelsior lots had been entered by one vendor and it was becoming obvious there was more to this than met the eye. As mentioned earlier in the text, the crankcase of BRBR101/S looked odd, but Dave found a notebook that belonged to his uncle and this bike and engine BRBR100 were both made with the old style low crankcase. (The new type was not back from machining in time for the show). The bike was evidently the 1938 Show bike and the front engine plates still show chrome on from the show.

I have slotted the bike in this section because, to keep it up to date, there has been a swinging arm fitted; the front forks have had an enclosed centre spring added.

I spoke to the good lady about this and was told to go for it! The only way to sort everything out was to buy the lot and, as they say, the rest is history. What has come to light is that the rest of the lots turn out to be the S.R. West bike shown in the Keig collection, Volume 4, page 91. The late works tank on this bike had been shortened and fitted to the show bike to allow a Norton seat to be used. The bronze head engine was there in bits. A frame described as a works plunger (but which was in fact a rigid with a Norton set of plungers fitted and alloy covers to mimic Excelsior's) was in another lot.

Previously unknown bikes still turn up and, with the records and information held, we are able to authenticate them. So, if anyone out there has a BRBR type petrol tank on a shelf doing nothing, which would help to put the bike back to original, please get in touch.

THE MOTORCYCLE
EXHIBITION
EARLS COURT

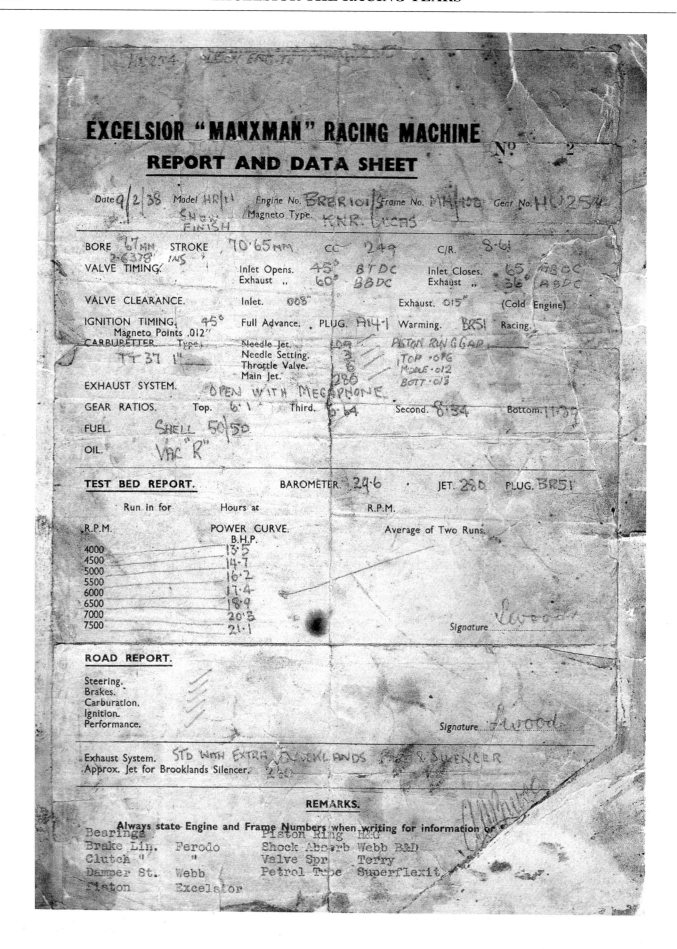

EXCELSIOR "MANXMAN" RACING MACHINE
REPORT AND DATA SHEET   Nº 2

Date 9/2/38   Model HR/11   Engine No. BRBR101   Frame No. MH100   Gear No. HU254
SNOW   Magneto Type. KNR. LUCAS
FINISH

BORE 67MM   STROKE 70·65MM   CC 249   C/R. 8·61
2·6378 INS
VALVE TIMING.

	Inlet Opens.	45°	BTDC	Inlet Closes.	65° ABDC
	Exhaust „	60°	BBDC	Exhaust „	36° ABDC

VALVE CLEARANCE.   Inlet. 008"   Exhaust. 015"   (Cold Engine)

IGNITION TIMING. 45°   Full Advance.   PLUG. A14·1   Warming. BR51   Racing.
Magneto Points .012"

CARBURETTER   Type.   Needle Jet.   PISTON RING GAP
TT 37 1"   Needle Setting. 3   TOP ·016
   Throttle Valve. 6   MIDDLE ·012
   Main Jet. 280   BOTT ·013

EXHAUST SYSTEM.   OPEN WITH MEGAPHONE

GEAR RATIOS.   Top. 6·1   Third. 6·64   Second. 8·34   Bottom. 11·37

FUEL. SHELL 50/50

OIL. VAC "R"

TEST BED REPORT.   BAROMETER. 29·6   JET. 280   PLUG. BR51

Run in for   Hours at   R.P.M.

R.P.M.	POWER CURVE. B.H.P.	Average of Two Runs.
4000	13·5	
4500	14·7	
5000	16·2	
5500	17·4	
6000	17·4	
6500	18·9	
7000	20·3	
7500	21·1	

Signature   Wood

ROAD REPORT.

Steering.
Brakes.
Carburation.
Ignition.
Performance.

Signature   Wood

Exhaust System.   STD WITH EXTRA BROOKLANDS & SILENCER
Approx. Jet for Brooklands Silencer. 240

REMARKS.

Always state Engine and Frame Numbers when writing for information or

Bearings		Piston Ring	H&G
Brake Lin.	Ferodo	Shock Absorb	Webb B&D
Clutch "	"	Valve Spr	Terry
Damper St.	Webb	Petrol Tube	Superflexit
Piston	Excelsior		

Nice shot showing a Manxman engine in a Norton chassis.

This is a shot of T.W. Swarbrick, on the left, from the Preston & D.M.C. He ran a converted swinging arm Manxman in the 1949 Clubman TT Races and, after a bit of trouble getting going, managed to finish twelfth. This bike turned up several years ago not twenty miles from the Preston area and is now in the south of England awaiting attention.

Some of the programmes of races where individuals mentioned in this book have appeared and letterheads

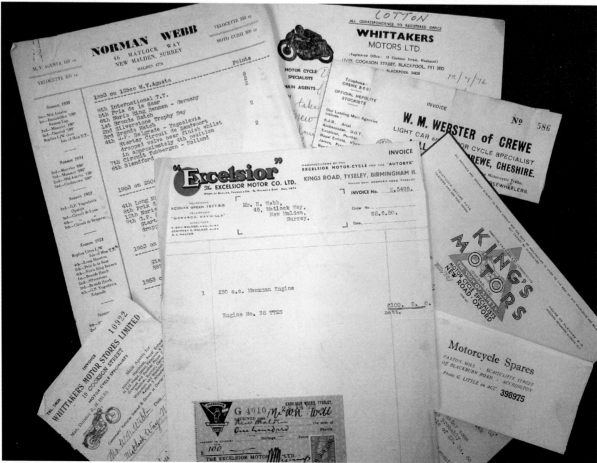

250 & 350 c.c. O.H.C. "MANXMAN" RACING Models
GENUINE RACING MACHINES—NOT REPLICAS

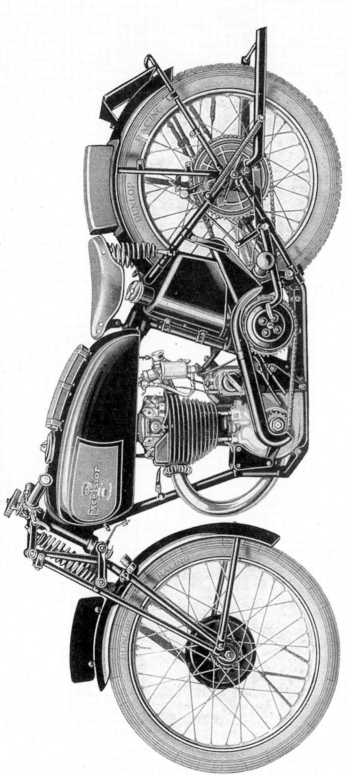

The machines which at their FIRST appearance WON at RECORD SPEEDS the NORTH-WEST 200 (250 c.c. class), the SOUTH AFRICAN DURBAN-JOHANNESBURG ROAD RACE and the WEST AUSTRALIAN T.T. against ALL COMERS.

These real racing models are supplied with full road-racing Equipment, and with special specification for Grass track racing. We invite all enthusiasts to apply for the detailed Specifications, given fully upon request.

Abridged Specification :—
Genuine **Racing "Manxman"** Engine with Aluminium **Bronze** head, polished ports, special **racing** cams and valves and high compression **racing** piston. Four speed special racing footchange gearbox (No kick-starter).
Lucas racing magneto (Laboratory tested).
A.M.A.L. special racing Carburetter.
Webb Racing Forks with shock absorbers and steering damper.
7" T.T. Brakes with special alloy shoes.
Dunlop Racing Tyres.
Large capacity separate Petrol and Oil Tanks.
Bi-Metal heads and Cylinders available at extra charge.

250 c.c. Model F.R.11 -
350 c.c. Model F.R.12 -

Note.—All "Manxman" Models are delivered suitable for running on 50/50 Petrol-Benzol fuel. A **rev. counter** graduated to 8,000 and with built-in drive to engine positively lubricated can be supplied with instrument mounted in tank at an extra charge of

FR11 and FR12 racing models

ROAD RACING MODELS—**GENUINE RACING MACHINES**—NOT REPLICAS.

SPECIFICATION

250 c.c.
Model G.R.11

Code Word :
" RACER "

350 c.c.
Model G.R.12

Code Word :
" RACAN "

ENGINE—Excelsior Special Racing. Model G.R.11, Bore 67 m/m, Stroke 70.65 m/m=248.6 c.c. Model G.R.12, Bore 75 m/m, Stroke 79 m/m=349 c.c. Overhead Camshaft. Vertical Shaft Bevel Gear driven. Entire mechanism totally enclosed. Alloy Bronze Cylinder Head. Down-draught Inlet. Large diameter Valves—special material. Valve Springs—Triple (Terry " AERO " quality). Camshaft on two Roller and one Ball Journal. Cams on Taper and detachable. Rockers in K.E. steel on hardened Spindles and Needle Rollers. Vertical Shaft on self-aligning Ball Journals. Hardened Iron Cylinder Barrel, ground and lapped bore. R/R alloy heat-treated Con-rod. Big End Sleeve shrunk in and ground in position. R/R alloy heat-treated Slipper Piston. Hollow 23/32" diameter Gudgeon pin, 250 c.c., ⅞" diameter on 350 c.c., fully floating in Piston. High tensile Flywheels forged with integral large diameter Mainshafts. Whole assembly machined, ground and balanced dynamically and statically. Drive Side Main Bearing—Hoffman Special Double Row Roller. Dural Cage. Timing Side Main Bearing—Double Ball Journal. Gear Drive to Oil Pump and Magneto, incorporating built-in and positively lubricated Revolution Counter Gear Box.

EXHAUST SYSTEM—Open pipe of correct length and bore to give maximum efficiency. Chrome-plated. No silencer.

LUBRICATION—High level double gear Oil Pump. Large diameter flexible feed and filter to Pump. ½" diameter Flexible Pipe carries surplus oil externally direct to the Timing Case and Sump where, with surplus oil from Big End, Cylinder and Piston it collects in Sump at a level below Flywheels (preventing oil drag). Suction Pump picks up oil and returns it to tank at a point visible at Filler Cap.

OIL CIRCULATION—17 gallons per hour at 7,000 r.p.m.

CRADLE FRAME—" A " quality steel tubes throughout. Single top tube 1½" diameter. Large webbed Steering Head. 1⅜" diameter Front Tube.

GEAR BOX—" Excelsior " Albion 4-speed T.T. Ball Bearing Gear Box, pivot mounted. K.E. Gears and Shafts. "Excelsior" exclusive positive operation, short travel Foot Change by Heel and Toe pedal. No Kick-start.

FORKS—Genuine T.T. Forks. Central compression spring rubber mounted. Single sided, adjustable, Shock absorber. Built-in Steering Damper.

REVOLUTION COUNTER—Fitted as standard to all Racing " MANXMAN " Models. Constructed with **built-in** gear drive to engine, positively lubricated, and graduated to 8,000 r.p.m.

IGNITION—Lucas laboratory tested Racing Magneto.

CARBURETTER—T.T. "AMAL" Needle Type. Large single float chamber independently mounted. Feed by twin armoured flexible pipes.

TRANSMISSION—Primary Chain. ½" x .305". Steel chrome-plated Chain-guard. Positive adjustable Oil Feed. Rear Chain : 250 c.c., ½" x .305". 350 c.c., ⅝" x ¼".

WHEELS and BRAKES—7" diameter x 1¼" Brakes. Light alloy die-cast Shoes mounted on alloy anchor and side plate, with over-hung Cam Bearing. Light Steel Rims. Double butted Spokes. Front tyre : 250 c.c., 27" x 2.75", Ribbed Road Racing ; 350 c.c., 27" x 3.00", Ribbed Road Racing. Rear Tyre : 250 c.c., 26" x 3.00" Studded Road Racing ; 350 c.c., 26" x 3.25", Studded Road Racing. All Racing " MANXMAN " Tyres are fitted by the **Dunlop Racing Tyre Fitters.**

FUEL TANK—3½ gallon steel-welded and rivetted construction throughout. Completely insulated from vibration on Rubber Mountings. Large quick-action T.T. Filler Cap. Revolution Counter, well built in and Sponge Rubber Pad fitted. Finish : Black Enamel with Red side panels. (No Knee Grips).

OIL TANK—8 pints. Quick action Filler Cap on near side. Detachable Oil Filter. Pressure Release Pipe leading to Chains.

SADDLE—DUNLOP RACING SADDLE.

MUDGUARDS—In accordance with F.I.C.M. regulations, with built-in racing number plate mounting. Fitted with T.T. Mudguard Pad.

ADJUSTABLE RACING FOOTRESTS. INDEPENDENT BRAKE PEDAL STOP. Tools and Pump included, also Spare Jets, Racing 14 m/m Plug Spanner and Racing Plug.

Special 250 c.c. Engine. Bi-Metal Cylinder Head and Cylinder, giving additional cooling, high compression, greater power and speed, at the same time reducing weight. extra. **Brooklands Silencer** extra. **Special 350 c.c. Engine with Bi-Metal Cylinder Head only** giving above advantages extra.

Page Six

GR11 and GR12 racers

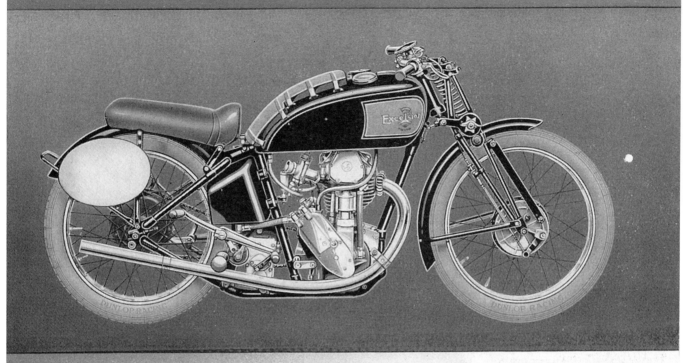

250 c.c & 350 c.c "RACING MANXMAN"

ROAD RACING MODELS—GENUINE RACING MACHINES—not replicas, every Model built and tested by our Racing and Experimental Department.

SPECIFICATION

250 c.c.
Model H.R.11

Code Word :
" RACER "

£95 - 0 - 0

350 c.c.
Model H.R.12

Code Word :
" RACAN "

£100

Page Six

ENGINE—Excelsior Special Racing. Model H.R.11, Bore 67 mm. Stroke 70.65 mm.=248.6 c.c. Model H.R.12, Bore 75 mm. Stroke 79 mm.=349 c.c. Overhead Camshaft. Vertical Shaft Bevel Gear Driven. Entire mechanism totally enclosed. Aluminium Bronze Cylinder Head. Down-draught Inlet. Large diameter special material Valves. **Hairpin Valve Springs.** Camshaft on two Roller and one Ball Journal. Cams on Taper and detachable. Rockers in K.E. steel on hardened Spindles and Floating Bronze Bushes. Vertical Shaft on self-aligning Ball Journals. **Hardened Iron Cylinder Barrel,** ground and lapped bore. R/R Alloy heat-treated Con-rod. Big End Sleeve shrunk-in and ground in location. Special Alloy heat-treated Slipper Piston. Hollow Gudgeon Pin fully floating in Piston. High tensile steel Fly-wheels forged with integral Mainshaft. Whole assembly machined, ground and balanced. Drive Side Main Bearing—Hoffman Special Double Row Roller. Timing Side Main Bearing—Double Ball Journal. Gear Drive to Oil Pump and Magneto, incorporating built-in and positively lubricated Revolution Counter Gear Box.

EXHAUST SYSTEM—Open pipe of correct length and bore to give maximum efficiency. Chrome-plated. No silencer.

LUBRICATION—High level double gear Oil Pump. Large diameter flexible feed and filter to Pump. ⅜" diameter Flexible Pipe carries surplus oil externally direct to the Timing Case and Sump where, with surplus oil from Big End, Cylinder and Piston it collects in Sump at a level below Flywheels (preventing oil drag). Suction Pump picks up oil and returns it to tank at a point visible at Filler Cap.
OIL CIRCULATION—17 gallons per hour at 7,000 r.p.m.

CRADLE FRAME—"A" quality steel tubes throughout. Single top tube 1¼" diameter. Large webbed Steering Head. 1⅜" diameter Front Tube.

GEAR BOX—Excelsior Albion 4-speed T.T. Ball Bearing Gear Box, pivot mounted. K.E. Gears and Shafts. **Excelsior** exclusive positive operation, short travel Foot Change by Heel and Toe pedal. No Kick-start.

FORKS—Genuine T.T. Forks. Central compression spring rubber mounted. Single sided, adjustable, Shock absorber. Built-in Steering Damper.

REVOLUTION COUNTER—Fitted as standard to all Racing "MANXMAN" Models. Constructed with **built-in** gear drive to engine, positively lubricated, and graduated to 8,000 r.p.m.

IGNITION—Lucas laboratory tested Racing Magneto.

CARBURETTER—T.T. "AMAL" Needle Type. Large single float chamber independently mounted. Feed by twin armoured flexible pipes.

TRANSMISSION—Primary Chain, ⅜"×.305". Steel chrome-plated Chain-guard. Positive adjustable Oil Feed. Rear Chain : 250 c.c., ½"×.305". 350 c.c., ⅝"×¼".

WHEELS and BRAKES—7" diameter × 1¼" Brakes. Light alloy die-cast Shoes mounted on alloy anchor and side plate, with over-hung Cam Bearing. Light Steel Rims. Double butted Spokes. Front tyre : 250 c.c., 27"×2.75", Ribbed Road Racing ; 350 c.c., 27"×3.00", Ribbed Road Racing. Rear Tyre : 250 c.c. 26"×3.00" Studded Road Racing ; 350 c.c., 26"×3.25", Studded Road Racing. All Racing "MANXMAN" Tyres are fitted by the Dunlop Racing Tyre Fitters.

FUEL TANK—3¼ gallon steel-welded and rivetted construction throughout. Completely insulated from vibration on Rubber Mountings. Large quick-action T.T. Filler Cap. Revolution Counter, well built in and Sponge Rubber Pad fitted. Finish : Black Enamel with Red side panels. (No Knee Grips).

OIL TANK—8 pints Quick action Filler Cap on near side. Detachable Oil Filter. Pressure Release Pipe leading to Chains.

SADDLE—Special Combined Saddle and Mudguard Pad.

MUDGUARDS—In accordance with F.I.C.M. regulations, with built-in racing number plate mounting.

ADJUSTABLE RACING FOOTRESTS. INDEPENDENT BRAKE PEDAL STOP. Tools and Pump included, also Spare Jets, Racing 14 m/m Plug Spanner and Racing Plug.

SPECIAL NOTE.—Hairpin Valve Springs are Standard equipment on Model H.R.11. **Triple Coil Valve Springs** are Standard equipment on Models H.R.12. Hairpin Springs for H.R.12 £5 extra. Certain Bi-metal equipment is available at extra charges, full particulars and prices on application. **Brooklands Silencer and Pipe 30/- extra.**

SPEEDOMETERS—Unless otherwise ordered a Smith Illuminated Chronometric Trip Speedometer will be supplied at : ... ... **£2 15 0 extra**

HR11 and HR12 racers

250 c.c. J.R.11 and J.R.S.11

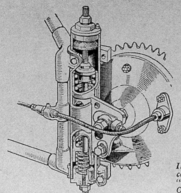

Illustration by the courtesy of "MOTOR CYCLING."

The rear Suspension and Girling brake.

Manxman

SPECIFICATION.

These models based on experience gained in the "T.T." and subsequently, have been almost completely re-designed, the two most important modifications being the arrangement of the engine and gear box to provide a semi-unit construction, and a fully enclosed duplex primary drive in a cast light alloy oil bath.

The rear suspension is basically that used in the "T.T." with two minor modifications. The re-bound is taken on coil springs, and the elimination of any possible shock through the suspension bottom on compression is provided for by two rubber buffers in the top end of the system. These will rarely come into use, as the amount of travel is adequate at 1.25".

Both capacities are also obtainable with the unit construction, but without the rear suspension.

Throughout the machine a special endeavour has been made to keep the weight within reasonable limits. The reduction or rather saving in weight is not obtained at the expense of the reliability of the various parts, which is entirely due to careful design and the use of the best quality light alloys, both in aluminium and steel.

THE FRAME of both models follows the well established and successful "Manxman" practice and incorporates cradle fixing for both engine and gear box. In addition, the engine is further secured to the frame high up at the front by two small triangular plates, the gear box bolting directly on to the rear of the engine and providing a three-point rigid fixing with the addition of a bolt through the cradle underneath the gear box and one to a lug on the saddle tube, forming what is to all intents and purposes, a unit.

THE REAR SUSPENSION is double plunger type, incorporating duplicated compression springs and re-bound springs.

The rear hub provides for the bearings to be very widely spaced and is so designed as to prevent the possibility of malalignment. The bearings are special Hoffmann Journals, mounted on a spindle made from heat treated high tensile steel no less than .75" diameter being provided with safety adjustments, which in addition to the nuts secure the wheel rigidly between the two plungers. The features of the suspension are simplicity combined with immense strength.

The frame itself has all joints brazed, the lugs being made from 20-ton castings. The tubing is 531 quality throughout, and is finished with dead hard stove black enamel.

FRONT FORKS are "T.T." WEBB with built in shock absorber and steering damper. There is also provision for a fork buffer to prevent the possibility of bottoming. Racing number plate fixings are also provided.

TANKS. Both fuel and oil tanks are hand-made from high tensile steel, all joints being welded and subsequently annealed before finishing in stove black enamel with red panels. Fuel tank capacity is 4 gallons. Oil tank capacity 1 gallon. Both are provided with pressure release pipe and the mountings are arranged to completely isolate the tanks from vibration or shocks. **Smith's Rev. Counter,** which is standard equipment, is mounted in the front right-hand side of the fuel tank, being balanced on the near side by a large diameter quick action "T.T." filler cap. The oil tank has a similar filler cap slightly smaller.

MUDGUARDS are dimensioned to comply with the F.I.C.M. Competition Regulations, the metal being steel; stays are steel and light alloy.

HANDLEBARS. Fully adjustable with large clutch and brake levers. Positive stop twist grip throttle control and the usual ignition and air controls. Bowdenex cable is used throughout.

REAR HUB has already been mentioned and the front has similar bearings but of slightly smaller dimensions, spindle being high tensile steel. Both wheels fitted with 7" **Girling** brakes, cable operated, provided with simple positive adjustments. Brake mechanism enclosed by elektron plates, the front being fitted with air intake and exit which provides draught, maintaining the condition of the linings and the drum. The linings themselves are "FERODO." Total braking area is 30 square inches. Rear brake is pedal operated on the near side and the front brake by lever on the off side of the handlebar.

SADDLE is the now familiar type combined with the rear pad. It is mounted on a light steel frame with Dunlopillo covered with black leather, and the fixing is rigid.

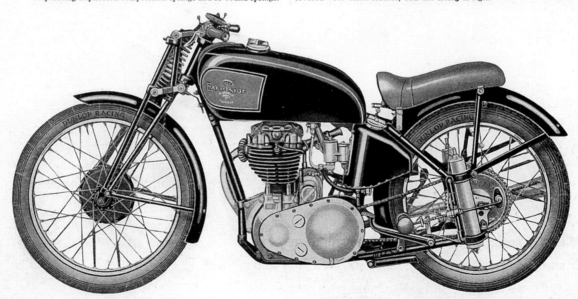

ROAD RACING MODELS—GENUINE RACING MACHINES—not replicas; every Model built and tested by our Racing and Experimental Department.
Page EIGHT

JR11 and JRS11 racers

Works Bikes

1929 250 cc JAP engined racers

Four bikes were entered in the 1929 TT and Crabtree won. One bike is known to exist and is shown in the book.

Marvels

The 1933 bikes were broken up, the engines and gearboxes were fitted into the new 1934 chassis, of which six are known to have been ordered. Crabtree's frame was cut up after his crash and the parts put back in the stores and Norman Webb was known to have built one of the old 1933 bikes, having found a chassis and using one of his spare engines.

1 bike is in the Sammy Miller museum.

2 bikes are in the National museum in Birmingham

1 bike is in the USA.

1 bike, the Sorensen machine shown on the rear cover of this book, is in private hands.

1 bike, the Ronnie Mead machine, is in the Hockenheim museum

Extra engine spares were made and perhaps there is another out there

Works Manxman

1935

Six bikes were made with elektron crankcases and left hand port heads.

The Manders bike is in Australia.

A second bike is in South Africa

It is not known at the moment if any others survive.

1936 and 1937 four valve bikes

Six bikes were built and spare four valve top ends were produced. In 1938 the engines were broken up to re-use the elektron crankcases in the spring frame bikes for that season. I would think the old chassis would have had two valve engines fitted and sold off to favoured riders.   When Norman Webb bought out the race shop he received all the top ends and spares.

1 cambox and head went to Germany and was built into a bike.

1 cambox and head went to New Zealand and was built into a bike.

1 cambox and head was sold in England and built into a bike

1 bare head went to the Lincoln area.

Norman Webb built two bikes, both of which are now on display in the National.

1 unfinished bike went through the Autokraft auction and is in private hands.

1938 bikes

6 semi-unit plunger bikes.

1 semi-unit rigid bike.

1 long rigid bike with the same forks, tanks and wheels as the semi-unit bikes. This was a works practice bike and then went to Sorensen.

1 pre-unit 500 cc plunger.

1 rigid pre-unit for Cadman, later altered by the factory to plunger.

The 500 plunger bike is in Australia.

2 semi-unit plunger bikes are in the National.

2 semi-unit plunger bikes are in private hands.

1 semi-unit plunger is in the USA.

The rigid semi-unit bike is in private hands.

The Sorensen long rigid is in private hands.

The Cadman bike is in private hands.

Other works bikes

Over the period the factory also made various other development bikes and the one-off ISDT Trials bike.

The ISDT bike is in private hands and none of the other development bikes, to my knowledge, have turned up yet. If you own a special Manxman then get in touch and I will amend my records.

Replicas

Two pre-unit replica plunger bikes are known to have been made. Alan Bruce was helping someone in Germany to build one, and I let someone in New Zealand have one of the special springer brake plates, to enable him to convert a rigid bike. He sent me photos of the bike being built.

Duplicated numbers

Some of the production racers share the same engine number. In the odd case I have no doubt that someone has decided to build himself a racer and altered or re-stamped a number. I have seen altered numbers on a few engines.

But the most likely reason for duplication is that, when racing on the Continent, a carnet was required for border crossings. The factory and some racers numbered their spare engine the same as those on the complete bikes in order to get around the problem.

Another reason is that, when an engine blew up, the factory supplied new cases numbered from their records. As spares became scarce and welding techniques improved, the broken cases were repaired, leading to bikes with the same engine number.

Technical information

Taken from the 1935 Excelsior handbook.

TECHNICAL DATA

Model	Bore m.m.	Stroke m.m.	Displacement c.c.	Compression Ratio	Weight complete	B.H.P.	R.P.M.	Approx. Fuel & Oil Consumption		Spark Plug Fitted Standard	Alternative Recommendations
								Fuel	Oil		
E11	63	79	247.7	7.5		17	6500	85	2000	Lodge H.53	K.L.G. 831LR
F11	63	79	247.7	7.5		17.5	6500	85	2000	R.14	831 or LB1
E12	75	79	349	7.25		21.5	6000	80	2000	H.53	831 or LB1
F12	75	79	349	7.25		22	6000	80	2000	R.14	831 or LB1
F14	82	94	496.6	7	350	30	5250	75	1750	R.14	831 or LB1
ER11	63	79	247.7	10	298	22	7250	45	750	warming H.53 Racing BR51	B831LB warming B731 racing
FR11	67	70.5	248.6	9.5	295	22.5	7350	45	750	warming A14-1 Racing BR51	B831 warming B731 racing
ER12	75	79	349	9	310	28	7000	40	750	warming H.53 Racing BR51	B831LR warming B731 racing
FR12	75	79	349	8.75	300	29	7000	40	750	warming A14-1 Racing BR51	B831LR warming B731 racing

TECHNICAL DATA

Model	Valve Timing				Valve Clearance Engine Cold		Ignition Timing	Chain Sizes		Carburetter Type	Standard Jet
	Inlet		Exhaust		Inlet	Exhaust		Front	Rear		
	Opens	Closes	Opens	Closes							
E11 ...	35°	60°	62°	20°	.008	.002	42	½ × .305	½ × .305	Amal 76/109	130
E12 ...	35°	55°	60°	21°	.008	.004	42	½ × .305	⅝ × ¼	Amal 76/112	150
F11 ...	35°	60°	62°	20°	.008	.004	42	½ × .305	½ × .305	Amal 76/109	130
F12 ...	40°	62°	62°	34°	.008	.004	42	½ × .305	⅝ × ¼	Amal 76/111	150
F14 ...	44°	55°	62°	38°	.008	.004	40	½ × .305	⅝ × ¼	Amal 89/014	170
ER11 ...	35°	55°	60°	25°	.008	.004	42	½ × .305	½ × .305	Amal 15 TT34	250
ER12 ...	40°	55°	62°	21°	.008	.004	40	½ × .305	⅝ × ¼	Amal 10 TT34	270
FR11 ...	40°	62°	62°	35°	.008	.004	40	½ × .305	½ × .305	Amal 15 TT35	240
FR12 ...	40°	62°	62°	35°	.008	004	40	½ × .305	⅝ × ¼	Amal 10 TT35	270

We have found that, on the BRAR 1936 series, most engines had left hand port heads. These we think are the early BRR optional bi-metal heads. In the 1937 series we have only found one left hand port recorded the rest known are right hand.

From 1935 to 1939 there were four separate crankcase re-designs.

Early engines measured 63 x 79 mm (250 cc) and 75 x 79 mm (350 cc).
Later engines measured 67 x 70.65 mm (250 cc) and 75 x 79 mm (350 cc).

The production racers used a 1"3/4 diameter exhaust system. The works racers used a smaller bore exhaust.

At least two of the later bikes came from the factory in the old Marvel silver and red colours. Whether this was a special order, we do not know. The standard colour scheme was black and red.

It must be noted that the catalogues cannot be relied on for exact specifications; they can be used only as guides.

From the Amal catalogue, information on racing Manxman carburetters:

Year	Model	Carb	Size	Jet	Throttle Valve	N/dl position	F/Chamber angle
1935	ER11	15TT34	1"	250	5	5	20%
1935	ER12	10TT34	1" 1/16	270	4	4	20%
1936	FR11	15TT35	1"	250	5	5	20%
1936	FR12	10TT35	1" 1/16	270	4	4	20%
1937	GR11	15TT35	1"	250	5	5	20%
1937	GR12	10TT35	1" 1/16	310	4	4	20%
1938	HR11	15TT36	1"	260	5	5	15%
1938	Option	15TT37RN	15/16	300	5	4	15%
1938	HR12	10TT36	1" 1/16	390	4	4	15%

REDFERN ROAD WORKS.   (Established 1874.)   KING'S ROAD WORKS.

Head Office & Works : KING'S ROAD, TYSELEY, BIRMINGHAM
NEAREST STATION: TYSELEY (GREAT WESTERN RAILWAY)

Telephone : 277-8 Acock's Green.   Telegrams : "Monarch, Hay Mills."   Code : A.B.C. 5th Edition.